I0059323

"Down to earth, practical information that will help any marketer make much better use of the social media revolution. I highly recommend it."
   - Al Ries, best selling author of *War in the Boardroom*

"This is one of the most insightful business books you'll read. It's thorough, interesting, easy to read, and clever. Spending time with "Friends with Features and Benefits" is the best investment you could make in your business this year."
   - Lon Safko, best selling author of *The Social Media Bible* and *Fusion Marketing Bible*

"A great look at the promises and pitfalls of social media. Real life examples, insightful concepts and easy-to-implement strategies give marketers the guidance they need to run successful social media programs."
   - Jim Kukral, author of *Attention, This Book Will Make You Money*

Friends With Features & Benefits

A Marketer's Guide to Scoring with Social Media

Kenneth J. Weiss

Copyright © 2013 by Kenneth J. Weiss. All rights reserved.
Published by About 360 Studio.

ISBN
978-0-615-82258-7

Library of Congress Control Number
2012901963

No part of this book may be used or reproduced in any manner without written permission except in the case of quotations used in articles and reviews. Any person committing an unauthorized act may be liable to criminal prosecution and civil claims for damages.

This book may be purchased for educational, business, or promotional use. For more information contact the author, KennethJWeiss@gmail.com.

Forward

Brands and consumers are hooking up. Social media is one giant love fest. Will it last, or is the fling enough?

Let me start by saying that I am a huge believer in social media. It's hot. Everyone wants to do it, and I want brands to embrace social media. However, some of the content in this book will challenge the applicability of social media and the path many companies are taking. Why? I was around during the emergence of online advertising in the 90's. Some groups in the online community did it a disservice by over-promising and under-delivering. Companies raced online, and as the space became congested, performance declined. Brands scoffed and retreated. Online advertising was a victim of its own limited set of metrics and it took a few years for the industry to recover.

This time around, the believers, the skeptics and those on the sidelines need to be better informed. Social media allows marketers to tell a story, build a brand, and connect with customers like nothing else.

It can feel great if you do it right.

Special thanks to my editors Mark, Barbie and Allie. Once again, I could not have done it without you.

Contents

Chapter 20

It Might Feel Funny

You'll feel funny, but you need to get started
129

Chapter 1

Not Just Videos, Pics and Pick Ups

Expand your definition of social media to include more than just the leading sites and apps

When the typical executive is asked to define social media, they will usually reference YouTube, Facebook, Twitter and other popular properties. This is a reasonable starting point. After all, these sites get a lot of love in the media, and they garner a huge percentage of traffic in the social world. However:

In order to understand social media you need to look beyond the brands and buzz to the core functionality. The names of sites will change, and new sites will come and go. Sites will alter their business models and invent new technologies. At the most fundamental level, though, you will find a tool set that allows brands and consumers to hook up: to discuss, to connect, to create and to share.

Social media is not one thing, but hundreds of experiences that are fueled by people's desires to communicate and

1

deliver their personalities, interests and daily life in the new digitally enabled world.

In order to use social media, a business must realize that traditional business practices still stand: have an objective, develop the strategies, and only then select the tactics. You can't hurry to tactics and hope to be satisfied. In some instances YouTube, Twitter and Facebook will be the answer. In other situations you will need to look across the broad spectrum of sites and apps in the social media space and select the key ones, or create a pallet of solutions that helps accomplish the objectives.

Let's take a look at what might be in the mix.

Social Networks

Social networks such as Facebook are usually a combination of capabilities rolled into a single user experience. Users can provide background information, add pictures, make recommendations, posts status updates and more. The key functionality is the ability to create networks joined by interests and friendships. Connected people or brands are continually fed a stream of information. Updates, posts and dynamic tidbits of mutual interest flow together seamlessly.

Special Interest Social Networks

Special interests networks attempt to define themselves around a smaller set of attributes. The forerunner in this space has been Linkedin. This network uses business relationships as the key factor. Other networks walk the fine line between being exclusive enough to be attractive while large enough to be an interesting and vibrant community.

2

Video Aggregation and Sharing

YouTube is the undisputed leader in the space. Users can upload videos, comment, share and more. As YouTube attempts to better monetize content, you will see changes in advertising formats, premium content and related services. Other video sites are attempting to split off lucrative niches by focusing on specific types of content, audiences and business needs such as training or troubleshooting videos.

Image Aggregation and Sharing

The explosion of digital cameras and mobile devices with cameras is creating an inexhaustible source of photos. Image editing software is becoming very inexpensive and in fact, can be found as a free download or a free service on the web. It is also a key element of brands like Instagram. These factors have driven the growth of sites where people can share, tag and distribute photos. Other social photo experiences like Pinterest allow users to collect images from the web, organize them and share them.

Blogging

Many internet historians view blogging as the technology that launched social media. In some respects, blogging is nothing more than the original promise of the web: the average person can publish online with little technical skill and have their ideas distributed to the masses. Today's blogging platforms allow people to publish all types of content, connect with other blogs, sell or syndicate advertising, distribute digital products and integrate with e-commerce platforms.

Micro Blogging and Statusing

Microblogging and statusing share the common characteristic of limiting the posts or information to a small blip. This can be the number of characters of text, size of images, length of video clip, etc. Twitter is the most common example. Following, tweeting and retweeting are now common activities in social media. Brands are having better luck fostering their own Twitter presence than trying to create advertising or sponsorship opportunities in another's social space.

Sharing your status is common in all types of social networks. This constant trickle of updates illustrates the nature and personality of a brand over time.

Peer-to-Peer Help Systems

As consumers have grown frustrated with the quality and availability of customer service from brands, they have increasingly turned to each other for help. Peer-to-peer help systems started as simple message boards and have evolved to complex communities with rating systems, sharing systems and more. In some industries, this type of help system is actively encouraged because it reduces costs and improves customer satisfaction. For other industries such as healthcare, insurance and finance, consumers advising other consumers can be dangerous.

Location, Trip And Travel

"Trip" has become a relative term. In today's digital world, a trip to the corner coffee shop now merits a posting. Location, trip and travel social experiences use geo-location technology, statuses, reviews, images and more to create interesting and sharable experiences.

4

Document Aggregation

Scribd and Slideshare have been the early leaders in the document aggregation space. In the past, companies cataloged documents, brochures, white papers and more on their own web sites. Users could certainly download the items, but the social experience was missing. Today, rating the items, offering comments and linking related works has made each piece of content more useful and valuable. The document owners benefit from more exposure. The downside, or upside, is that poor-quality documents will be identified quickly.

Events Scheduling and Sharing

Event scheduling sites and apps present easy and interesting ways to organize, promote, document and recap events. The social forces of seeing who is attending, reading comments, and seeing images is more persuasive than traditional scheduling tactics.

Music Sharing, Discovery and Distribution

The internet has changed the music industry more than any other industry and social media will continue the trend. Digital music is currency, entertainment and a cultural touch point. Social sites allow artists to cultivate their own audiences and create smaller and smaller niches. Music aggregation and community sites represent a new way of reaching consumers based upon complicated demographic, psychographic and affinity profiles.

Video and Audio Casting

Video and audio casting are primarily built around the streaming or distribution of live events. Events like the

Olympics and World Cup have shown that people can use the web and mobile devices to integrate the experience into their daily life, rather than arranging their life around the event. The newer formats include more than just the event itself. Real-time stats, commenting, expert blogging, fingertip research and other functionality provide new, configurable dimensions to the experience.

Social Bookmarking

Social bookmarking began as a simple function: a person could access bookmarks from any computer. It has evolved into a powerful system for sharing content, gathering likeminded people, fostering discussion and discovering (not just cataloging) new content.

Ratings and Reputation

One of the most compelling aspects of the social media space is the authority that is being developed by individual consumers. Some individuals have built powerful reputations in a particular hobby, business segment or knowledge slice. In other instances, a person's authority is situational. For instance, a person might have posted a rating or review of a particular hotel based upon a recent stay. Other consumers thinking about that hotel are now placing credence in the person and their review, while they may not find that person an authority on other subjects. A stunning amount of research now shows that people are more influenced by reviews and ratings from people "like them" than they are by the expert options of journalists or critics. For many companies and brands social media ratings and reviews are taken as the "unvarnished truth."

6

Crowdsourcing

Need an idea for a new product? Want a concept for a television spot? How about a different ending for a work-in-progress book? Ask the crowd! Crowdsourcing is used in the social media space as a form of distributed computing: put the task to hundreds or thousands of people, and wait for a better informed, more robust answer than the answer that would have sprung from traditional sources.

That's The Tool Set – Why Is It So Powerful?

Each of those social media elements is intriguing in its own right, but a series of common characteristics create a scenario where the whole is greater than the sum of its parts.

- **Open** – Social media properties and platforms have developed a philosophy that assures they will grow faster if other organizations are allowed to participate with meaningful business models. As a result, many social media properties are no longer walled gardens. Outside organizations contribute to the maturation of the property and its attractiveness to the marketplace through win-win investments.

- **Interconnected** – Being connected is really at the heart of social media for users, and the same sentiment is at work in social media properties. Functionality and features of one social property often appear in their branded format on other properties.

- **Blended** – Very few social sites are pure plays of a single capability. While a property may promote a core functionality, it is usually enhanced with sharing, commenting and community functions.

- **Portable** – The growth of smart phones and the Internet connectivity of gaming systems is teaching the world that true user experiences are not dependent upon a single device type. Research indicates that mobile devices will soon overtake PCs as the preferred method for interacting with social properties.

- **Friction Free** – Technology, connectivity and vast improvements in usability and user experience strategy have lead to a point in time where social media properties are easy to use. An individual can participate in almost any aspect of the social world with little training and almost no barriers to entry.

- **User Directed (Within Confines)** – Do you remember MySpace when it was the darling of the social media world? Viewing a selection of My Space profiles was like a trip through a post-apocalyptic, digital year book from Mad Max High. Music blared. Graphics blinked. Private parts were everywhere. The social space quickly realized that giving users huge amount of control and a voice in the product had its limits. Social media properties operate under a spirit that puts user's decisions first, but only within the confines of policies, brand and user experience.

So That's Social Media? Nothing Else?

Defining social media is never a completed project. If you consider the rapid, and now historic, emergence of Flickr, MySpace, YouTube and Pinterest, you'll realize that another major player is just around the corner. When you overlay the existing landscape with the dimensions of language, country, industry, demographics, psychographics, hobbies and interests, it's apparent that the number of combinations is endless.

8

Chapter 2

Be Bigger Than Just Social Media

Social media is only part of a larger digital marketing strategy

Businesses are concentrating on social media. It's fun. It gets attention. It gets you attention. But – it is only a part of a complete digital strategy. Companies need to start at the top by defining long term marketing objectives and then decide how digital can play a role, and what tactics should be engaged. Those tactics may or may not include social media.

The Big Picture: E-Business, E-Marketing, E-Commerce and E-Service

E-Business is a big concept that is probably shared by many portions of the organization including operations, finance, sales, IT and marketing. Today, e-business is about breaking down walls of the organization, and then extending electronic relationships deeper into the supply chain and further into the distribution channel. Thinking of creating a distance learning system so the training time for the rep force is greatly reduced? That's good e-business. Want to create an enhanced on-boarding program for new employees that includes web videos, communities and profiles? That's e-business with social media components.

E-Marketing is shared by marketing, sales, product development, brand, public relations, and more. This is where

9

social media is typically assigned within the organization. Although it is tempting to jump into social media, the organization needs to determine the opportunity cost of passing on other marketing projects.

The phrase "E-Commerce" was formerly reserved for the concept of selling products directly from a web site. The clear counterpart was selling items to another organization who would then sell them online. Today's correct use of "e-Commerce" includes these two and the vast space in between. Affiliate programs, marketplaces, auction sites, shopping engines, shopping apps and other blended transactional sites represent new models for the sale of goods. Many companies make the mistake of believing that simply upgrading their site to be e-commerce-enabled is the most significant milestone in the e-commerce journey. It's not. A company needs to look at the many channels within the e-commerce space and fully engage them all.

Sometimes Simple Is Better, Even If It Is Less Fun

Grunt work gets no glory, but many of these activities would provide a greater return on the investment, improve customer satisfaction more, and create better feelings toward the brand than social media.

- **Improved Image Galleries – Consumers are enamored with images. Talk to any major e-commerce organization and they will tell you that more images with more angles and more details sell product. Not only do consumers want more images, but they also want zoom features and the ability to see products in different colors and sizes. They even want to see products in different combinations and in different settings.**

10

- More Video Content – We are living in a video world. Consumers and business users of web content want to see video. If a picture is worth a thousand words, a video is worth a million. Web video technology has improved to the point where it is almost 100% error-free. "Not being able to watch the video" is no longer a justifiable excuse.

- Improved Self-Service Resources – Sometimes consumers don't want to be dazzled. Sometimes they just want simple answers. Where's the instruction manual? How do I troubleshoot an issue? Which of your products work together? What kind of cleaning solution goes in this unit? Can I use a different brand with yours? Offering a simple, clear answer that provides certainty is essential. When a consumer is informed and confident, they will build a stronger relationship with the brand.

- Improved Product Presentation on Partner Sites – Have you ever conducted a thorough audit of how your products or services are displayed on partner sites or distribution channel sites? Right photos? Correct copy? Is everything complete? Any competing products presented in a different manner? A better manner? Can you answer these questions? Probably not. Very few companies regularly spend the time and effort required to do a complete job.

- A More Consistent Placement in Search Engines – Search engine optimization can be expensive and the "black magic" factor makes estimating ROI troubling. Search engines have also been known to make overnight changes to their algorithms which completely vaporize a site's listings. As scary as Search Engine Optimization (SEO) is, companies need to do it. SEO is not a one-time, quick fix solution. You need to take a hard look on an ongoing basis at the words and phrases that customers are using. You also need to be aware of the buzzwords being used in your space. It may be on-brand to refer to your products as

11

"dungarees" but customers are probably pounding the search engines with "jeans." So, create a list of the 50 most common words and phrases associated with your category. How many times do you come up on the first page? How many times are you in the top 3? How about #1?

- Complete and Accurate Web Copy – Complete and accurate are two different things. For many sites, the key products get attention and the others suffer. This is why you find some products with thorough descriptions complete with specs, installation information, etc, while others have a list of just a few bullets. Accuracy is another matter. If a packaging change was made, does the product image reflect the change? If a particular product was offered in three different sizes, but one has been dropped, does the site reflect the new offering? When a brand does a true, rigorous content audit, the number of discrepancies is often astounding.

- Bullet-Proof Usability – For many web sites, being original and interesting has trumped being usable. Big online retailers recognize the fallacy of this approach and have made usability a priority. Links look like links. Buttons look like buttons. Guiding, helping and informing the user are the driving factors. Almost every site can benefit from a usability assessment. This can be as simple as making sure forms are easy to use, and as complex as executing an audit to guarantee vision impaired users with special browsers are having a beneficial user experience.

- Improved Web Site Search – What's more important, posting a helpful tip each day on your Facebook page, or ensuring that customers on your site are actually finding the products they want when they search your site? Pretty obvious, isn't it? This doesn't always happen. Even the most basic search technology should be compensating for misspellings, omitted spaces, differences in vernacular and

12

brand/category terminology variances. A solid search technology should be showing related products, promoting specials and using popularity to shape results. When is the last time a search audit was done on your site? How many times is the "zero results" page generated each month? How often is the search results page the exit page for your site? Can't answer these questions? Search probably needs more attention.

- **Brand and IP Monitoring Strategies** – The internet is a very big place and is filled with lots of shady characters using other companies' brands and trademarks in bad ways. For example a company like XYZ Products probably has a web site called www.XYZProducts.com. What they many not realize is that the bad guys may have and endless slew of related urls in play such as DiscountXYZProducts.com, XYZProductOutlet.com, XYZ-Product-Sale.com and more. The bad guys may also be using the XYZ name in search engine marketing and as part of complex traffic routing schemes.

This is not to say that you should NOT embark on a social media program. You simply need to make sure that you are examining the relative merits of each digital opportunity.

Aside From Social Media, What Digital Topics Are Hot Right Now?

Not only is social media hot, but digital advertising, gaming, the mobile sphere, new device types, individual industries and specific tactics are red hot. Here just a few (of many) to ponder:

Connected Devices

E-readers, smart phones, web-enabled personal game systems, tablets, watches, health meters and multi-function music players redefine what it means to be connected to the web.

Pay-For-Performance Marketing

Paid search has been driving the online advertising industry for years. If you are not familiar with paid search it is pretty simple: An advertiser bids to have their listing appear on a search results page for a particular word or phrase, but only pays when the user clicks on their listing. This approach is now being used in many forms of online marketing. Advertising networks and sites are developing elaborate offerings where the advertiser only pays if a particular action is executed. This can be a click or a conversion. Tracking and attribution technologies are now strong enough that advertisers can bid with certainty.

Data Mining

The traditional worlds of direct mail, list services and data modeling are merging nicely into today's online world. Even if you only have a snippet of data about a user, third party services can append a sea of data to that starting point. The services can also use your existing internal data and third party data to create complex models of your customer base and industry.

Marketplaces

Many leading internet retailers have realized that their success has been due to the ability to create large, scalable systems and cultivate immense traffic bases. These two abilities are supercharging the growth of marketplaces. In a marketplace setting third party sellers are able to offer their goods within the context of the retailer's shopping experience. eBay led the way with "Buy It Now" pricing, and the Ama-

14

zon marketplace has helped accelerate the growth of the marketplace model. Unlike a traditional manufacturer/retailer relationship, a marketplace allows manufacturers to sell directly to consumers using the retailer's site as a conduit. The retailer never takes possession of the goods – they simply take a cut of the transaction. Retailers like the model because it allows them to monetize more of their traffic with little incremental overhead except for the cost of moving data.

Digital in Store

Retail stores are becoming increasingly wired. Point of sale systems are robust and serve as the tip of the spear in one-to-one marketing efforts. Kiosks are being integrated into store operations and marketing programs. Even traditional in-store marketing materials are being transformed into digital experiences. While all of these were experimental in the past, lower production costs, messaging flexibility, staff training and consumer acceptance of technology are creating positive ROI for digital in-store efforts.

UX as Part of the Product Offering

Using the web and kiosks has become commonplace when ordering airline tickets and processing digital photos at stores, but now we are seeing user experience (UX) being incorporated into all types of products and services. Data from digital pedometers can now be uploaded to a central workout tracker. GPS systems are built for dynamic updates. Diet programs combine retail food distribution with online calorie counting utilities. Kids' toys can be used in the real world and connected to a virtual world.

Geo-Targeting

Few people realize that all types of web and mobile traffic have an interesting layer of data running in the background: location information. Consumers know that if they provide a state or zip code to a site, they may see tailored information. That type of customized information, however, can be served to consumers without any user supplied data. As devices and browsers talk to systems, bits of behind-the-scenes information reveal the users' locations. Users see news, weather, sports, sales promotions and more that are specific to their location. Users are reacting favorably to this type of dynamic content and the models that govern the delivery are becoming more robust.

And, Don't Discount the Impact of a Really Strong Multi-Channel Strategy

The world is becoming more digital, but businesses are finding that the real bang can be found in online/offline hybrids. Several large retailers are combing their physical stores and web sites with site-to-store models. Conversely some stores offer the ability to buy at the store but have the order delivered to the customer's home. Online chat with a real customer service rep is becoming commonplace on web sites. Many e-commerce sites know that one of the most profitable ways to generate new customers is by sending traditional paper catalogs in the mail. Toll free phone numbers married to web systems are also a perennial favorite. Businesses need to take a hard look at their operations and determine if they have built silos or if they are developing a true multichannel strategy.

Chapter 3

You'll Spend More Than You Think

Social media requires more of an investment than you think

"Big budgets" and "small budgets" are relative terms. If you are a leading consumer packaged goods company or a brand that spends tens of millions each year in broadcast, dropping a few hundred thousand or even a million in social media is an afterthought. If you are a small regional retailer, a mid-sized B2B firm or a services firm that relies on word of mouth, spending a few thousand dollars for social media may require considerable thought.

Social media can be cost effective, but achieving critical mass is essential, and identifying the threshold for critical mass is not always possible.

Yes, Some of the Tools Are Free

Many social media tools are completely free, but like most businesses, social media outlets are always looking for ways to monetize their technology and user bases. So some social media sites will make divisions according to general or commercial usage, segment capabilities in free and paid tiers, or offer additional features that are designed to help your content, experience or profile bubble to the top. You-

Friends With Features & Benefits – A Marketer's Guide to Scoring with Social Media

Tube is a great example: Anyone can post videos, but a single video could be lost in the almost unimaginably large sea of videos that is YouTube. However, a brand can use any one of a number of programs available from YouTube to create custom experiences and promote videos if they are willing to pay.

The "Cheap" and Famous

Every now and then, a person or a brand breaks through the clutter and becomes an Internet sensation. Please remember, this is rare. This is not a strategy. Having this type of success is becoming more difficult because web users are more discerning, and the social media programs that are purely commercial in nature are viewed with some amount of disdain. People will forward "cool" stuff and talk about it. If it is a "sales pitch" - not so much. So let's look at a few people and brands that have made the social space work on a shoestring.

- **Cindy Margolis – Any good discussion of social media needs to include Margolis. Margolis was "viral" before people even used the term. In the early days of the web (think mid 1990's) Margolis was legendary for being the "most downloaded" person on the Internet. Her career exploded into international stardom that included film and television roles. Her path to fame clearly illustrates a key point: good content (in her case, pics of herself) is essential.**

- **The Dancing Baby – Ever heard of Michael Girard or Robert Lurye? Not many people have, but if you are a fan of Internet history you will remember a short animated clip produced by the duo that went crazy on the web in the 90s: "The Dancing Baby." The short, grainy clip featured a 3-D baby dancing. Yup. That's it. It was such a cul-**

18

tural touchstone, that the baby even made it into popular TV programs of the time. No brand. No dialogue. No graphics. Just a dancing baby. The lesson? You can never be sure what is going to strike a chord.

- The Evolution of Dance Guy – Unlike the Internet baby that never had a career after the first clip, entertainer Justin Laipply has been able to ride the viral wave of his clip "The Evolution of Dance" to a productive career. The original clip showed Laipply on stage dancing to various snippets of music. He was funny. How funny? It has been watched more than 150 million times! It was an unbelievable hit, and he was able to turn the interest into paying gigs.

- Blendtec – Blendtec reached the public consciousness through a series of "Will It Blend?" YouTube videos showing various items being pulverized in their blenders. Blendtec is no doubt the best early example of a brand using social media to promote its commercial mission. Along the way they took some smart and simple steps like looking at comments and requests to determine what would be blended next. The company was also able to ride other crazes to its advantage. Remember when Blendtec blended an iPhone the first day the device hit the market? It was a sensation. In the beginning it was truly low budget: the CEO Tom Dickson went on camera in a conference room and started blending different objects. Total cost? $50.

- Colbie Caillat and Justin Bieber – Not everyone who uploads a video to a social media property has become famous, but it has happened. And, for a select few, the proverbial "15 minutes of fame" has been usurped by substantial careers. Grammy Award winning artist Colbie Caillat got started by uploading videos to MySpace in 2005. What began as a few friends listening to her songs quickly turned into hundreds of thousands of friends and

19

millions of plays. Since then she has released numerous albums and is a fixture on the music scene. When Justin Bieber was only 12 his mother posted a few videos on YouTube which rapidly garnered millions of views. He went from being an unknown suburban kid to a hot prospect. Several of the biggest names in music aggressively pursued him. He eventually signed with Usher and Island Records. Both Beiber and Callait are well known names in their field, and both owe their fortunes to social media. The irony is that Callait has continued to rise while MySpace has faded. You can never be sure what will be a hit in the music biz, and social properties can follow the path of one hit wonders.

- **Various Twitter Accounts** – Twitter successes are numerous and the format, only 140 characters, means that people are on a more equal playing field when it comes to creating content. It is not hard to find stories of street vendors, comedians, haberdashers and other people who have made the combination of "where I am/what I'm doing" work for their business and their brand.

Do other "cheap" stories exist? Yes. Absolutely. Some are the stories of brands that have artfully navigated the social space and made it work on a shoestring. But for every one story of cheaply-gained business value, you will find dozens of instances of fleeting popularity. Remember the Star Wars Kid, the Numa Numa guy, quirk cars, fails and dancing wedding people? Yes? Some of them are hard to forget.

The "Not So Cheap and Famous"

Many brands have made an investment in social media and it has paid off. Other brands have made bigger investments, but have benefited far less. So, let's focus on the winners,

20

but remember throwing money at social media does not guarantee success.

Here are a few diverse examples (in no particular order) to illustrate what can be done.

- **Pepsi Refresh Everything** – Pepsi made huge news when it announced the decision to forgo advertising in the Super Bowl and instead use that money for social media programs. A big deal? Sure, Pepsi had been a Super Bowl advertiser for 23 years. Anyone remember the Cindy Crawford spot that revealed the new can? Ah, memories... Instead of 30 seconds of fun, Pepsi put $20 million behind the Refresh Everything project. $20 million! How does your t-shirt giveaway on Facebook feel now? Pepsi suits are quick to note that the program actually combines social media, TV, print, in-store elements and more in an integrated campaign.

- **Gatorade Ball Girl** – A little background: An internet clip showing a ball girl making a spectacular catch of a foul ball at a minor league baseball game went viral. The clip, which racked up millions of views, was quickly revealed as a hoax from the agency Element 79 intended to promote Gatorade. So what did it take to make it happen? A minor league baseball stadium, a professional stunt woman, support crew and special effects from a New York production company.

- **Ford Fiesta** – Ford built a successful social media program around the Ford Fiesta by giving 100 "agents" a free Ford Focus to drive. This was not a quick test drive. The lucky chosen ones could drive the car for up to six months. The agents were chosen to resonate with the target market, and for their ability to influence large social spheres. Two applicants had more the 30,000 MySpace friends. Eight had

21

more than 2,000 Facebook friends. Others were influential in blogs, on YouTube and had large Twitter followings.

- Barack Obama – Obama's first social media campaign is commonly regarded as the breakout example of social media being used as a weapon in the political process. On Election Day, Obama had 3 million supporters while McCain did not even crack the one million mark. Other numbers are just as staggering. Obama racked up 13 million names on the email list, 3 million online donors, 3 million opt-ins for text messaging and 2,000 official YouTube videos. All of this, however, was not a serendipitous groundswell of like-minded people. The social media campaign was a well-orchestrated and well-funded effort run by Chris Hughes, a co-founder of Facebook. The team operated from a Chicago headquarters with enough gear to make any dotcom start-up jealous. At its peak the campaign was spending more than $1 million per month on online advertising to drive supporters to MyBarackObama.com which garnered over 5 million visitor sessions per month.

- Old Spice – Great creative work and a now-legendary social media campaign made a stale brand hot again – just ask Old Spice. Ad firm Wieden + Kennedy created the Old Spice campaign around a former NFL player, Isaiah Mustafa. The campaign launched as an integrated campaign of web, media and TV elements. It was well done and not cheap. The real magic came from Isaiah himself. He was hilarious and worth the investment. The campaign reached its apex when the Old Spice guy began a rapid fire series of YouTube videos in response to Tweets. A team of social media experts, strategists, writers and video production pros gathered in a room and responded to the social stream with short videos. The team assessed the influence of the writers, the comments and the potential responses. The most notable series was a back-and-forth

22

social banter with Alyssa Milano. The effort was ramped down after several days, but will forever serve as a model of integration and rapid execution.

Are other people spending serious money? Absolutely. But, spending money is not a guarantee of success.

Get Ready For Prize Burnout

Our contest-promotion-event saturated world has seen just about everything: Win a walk-on role in a movie! Win a million bucks for answering a question! And on, and on. So, is it possible to offer a prize with a "wow factor?" Yes, but the prize needs to be impressive. If you do not understand the audience, you will not know how to push their buttons.

Consumers Understand Good Content and Experiences

Consumers are becoming very adept at sensing content that is new, original and valuable versus content that is low-budget, half-hearted and re-hashed. When a company has a belief that social media is free, the budget for content production is small, if not, non-existent. This "let them read cake" approach has the potential to create backlash rather than positive feedback.

Consumers also have an understanding of what represents a good experience. If your flash experience is supposed to be humorous, it better be as funny as the material on the comedy sites. If your game is supposed to be exciting, it better be as compelling as other high-end games. If your site is supposed to be helpful, it had better be created with a high level of usability.

Users know crap.

Even Really Great Social Media Programs Need An Integrated Push

Remember the old adage of a tree falling in the forest with nobody around? The same holds true for social media. If you have a really great social media experience but the audience is limited, did you really get the result you wanted?

This of course starts with defining the desired result. Far too many companies have aspirations of spreading their brand message to millions of new people using a social media strategy that focuses on the people already within their social sphere. Yes, people can be advocates of a brand, but that does not mean that they will push brand messages to everyone they know every day.

In order for social campaigns to rapidly gain traction and scale, online public relations, off line public relations, paid media and more need to be integrated within a carefully constructed launch plan.

Chapter 4

Social Media Has Moved In And Is Not Moving Out

Some sites and experiences may die, but social media is here to stay

If you have followed Internet business history for any period of time you know it has been a never-ending string of sure thing–can't miss–one hit wonder–next big thing–flash in the pan–where'd it go–IPO– uh, oh–gambles and guesses. Some sites start on a shoestring and hit it big. Others are started by smart folks with lots of funding and go absolutely nowhere.

Even now, many social media properties are building cult followings and amazing technology, but are struggling with that "little" problem of making money. But before you break out the CB radio analogies, rest assured social media is here to stay. The trick is to understand what the future holds and how the path from "now" until "then" will unfold.

Many Current Sites Will Not Survive

Many sites have managed to make it to profitability or have been purchased by deep-pocketed giants: think Flickr and YouTube. Others have enough funding to last almost indefinitely. However, many other sites and services in the social media space are engaged in a mad dash to some type of exit strategy. The sites may have some great technology and some people (excluding their parents and spouses) may think they are wonderful, but they will flat out not make it. Companies and brands should use them when prudent, but all eggs should not be placed in any of these fragile baskets.

New Sites, Services and Experiences Are Still To Come

The BTO fans know, "You ain't see nothing yet. Bbbbbaby, you ain't see nothing yet." Spend some time reading tech journals to see who is getting funded and which successful executives are chucking lucrative careers to jump into start-ups. It feels a lot like the Internet boom again.

Demographic Diversification Will Continue

Many kids say Facebook began to suck when their parents joined. For them it may be true, but people of all ages are discovering that social media is relevant to their relationships and lives. Seniors are using social media to stay in touch with relatives, old military buddies, grade school chums and retired colleagues. Media properties and brands are developing social experiences and games for children as young as three or four. As social media matures, usage among all segments will continue to increase. The properties and experiences used by each slice will be different, so understanding your audience will be important.

Streaming and Lifecasting Will Continue To Emerge

The line between status and streaming will get very thin for many social media users. Let's start with a little background: Many social media experiences allow you to provide a status. This is basically: "what I am doing right now." For some people, updating their status is a daily or weekly occurrence. For others, this is an almost non-stop process. Streaming and lifecasting represent a flow of non-stop data about a person. Some have done this as real time video

26

feeds: "Here's my life." "Watch our new house being built." Etc. Newer versions of this will tap into data that already exists but is not being exposed: "Track our college savings account." "Here is my gas mileage." "Follow my workouts." "Watch me keep track of my calories." In a world where transparency and privacy are rapidly changing, the possibilities are almost endless.

Gaming Integration Will Be A Social Force

Gaming, as an industry, has hit its stride in the past few years. Game releases like Madden Football and Call of Duty are now as big as movie releases. Game systems like the Wii and PSP have changed how people think about playing games and where they play them. This entire space is being complimented by online gaming, and games like Farmville, Mafia Wars, Angry Birds, Candy Crush and others have experienced periods of rabid popularity.

The integration is just getting started. When you consider the possibilities for gambling, fantasy sports, and more, it is easy to see how big this will be.

Content Will Get Richer

The web is bursting with rich content: flash, HTML5, video and dynamic experiences being delivered through full-throttle connection speeds. At home, game systems are delivering amazing graphics with lighting fast processors. The future combinations of rich content will be astounding.

Experience Segmentation Will Increase Within The Context of Large Networks

In the past, small networks and online communities have had mixed success. For example, support groups for people

27

with rare illnesses have survived because of the passion of the community. The users are committed and the subject matter is of great importance. Other groups for hobbies, odd genres of music and hyper-niche interests come and go. When there is no passion and no scale, the likelihood of success is limited.

In the future however, people will belong to niche groups within the context of their larger networks. The group will not have to create a separate social environment, rather it will be an environment within the context a larger social space. This arrangement will leverage existing technologies and allow people to be more casually interested.

Device Access and Device Integration Will Explode

Phones, MP3 players, game systems, flat panel televisions, and even connectivity services are being developed with integrated social media. "Integrate" probably does not do these new products justice. Everything about these devices – and others – is being re-imagined so that the new user experience is something different, not just an experience loaded with plug-ins.

Sharing, Piracy and Satire Will Be Tough To Sort Out

It's a wonderful time to be a content creator – and a pretty damn scary time, too. The save-cut-copy-paste world is now being made worse, or better depending upon your perspective, by a wide range of cheap and high powered DIY editing tools. Want to grab a snippet of a song? Want to put new subtitles to a movie clip. (Hitler meme fans raise your hand.) Want to snag a blog post and shill it as your own? All of these are easy and getting easier by the day. This is a slippery slope for brands, writers and artists. If artists attempt to mark their work in some sort of indelible way, people will be put off and less likely to share it. However, if content is left elegantly "unbranded" it can go viral or be ripped off and in neither case does anyone get credit.

Author's Note: I have found chunks of my previous book in blog posts, white papers and articles with absolutely no attribution. Flattering? Yes. Maddening? Yes.

Get Ready For More Professional Amateurs

Some people can really sing. Some can create amazing stories. Take great pictures. Make killer videos. Tell funny jokes. No doubt about it – the world has talent. Social media will allow more and more of these people to rise above the crowd to become professional amateurs. They may not ever reach celebrity "D-List" status. Heck, they may not ever crack the alphabet, but the power of social media will allow them to be tremendous influencers and to build their own brands.

Amanda Congdon and Perez Hilton are two archetypical personalities for this phenomenon.

Social Media Will Be Hooking Up Even More Often

Social media by nature is inherently connectable and modular. Some content types, industries and lifestyles are undeniably good fits, and we have, no doubt, only seen the surface being scratched.

- **Music – It's cool. The file sizes are small. MP3 players are cheap. Digital distribution is easy. Musicians tend to hang with other artist-types who can bring amazing visuals to the picture. Wow, what a recipe for a very bright future!**

- Journalism and News – When the tragic shootings at Virginia Tech took place in 2007 cell phone reporting was introduced into the journalism dialogue. Was it professional? No. Was it high quality? No. But, it was there. It was immediate. It was real. And chilling. News outlets now are embracing social media by asking people to provide first hand accounts, share images, upload videos and make comments.

- Reality TV – Just when you think every reality concept that exists has been tried; networks announce another round of shows. Cooking, shooting, modeling, designing and a hundred other talents are now part of the reality spectrum. People love talking about them and "creeping" on the contestants' Facebook pages. In the very near future, polls, voting and connecting will be even more integrated within the core concept of the shows.

- Customer Experience Strategy – Brands know that happy customers and disgruntled customer have always passed along their feeling to others. Social media supercharges that equation, so why not build those capabilities into the customer experience? Customer experience strategy goes beyond product design to include all of the different ways the item is shopped, purchased and serviced. Failure at any point on this continuum is fodder for social media discussion.

- Publishing – Traditional publishing is a tough business. The publisher must decide on whether to gamble on a long print run and reduce per unit costs, or print a shorter run to avoid getting stuck with inventory. Books are heavy and cumbersome to ship and store. On top of these factors, researchers suggest that people are reading less. But wait – how about those Harry Potter books? How does a publisher predict a hit like that? It's a tough business. Social media and the related digital devices are allowing new

30

publishing models to emerge. Print on demand solutions, pure digital publishing solutions, digital distribution and the ability of the social world will fuel new one-to-many and many-to-many marketing and publishing models.

- **Product Concepts And Solutions** – In the past few years the idea of crowdsourcing, allowing the wisdom of the crowds to generate ideas or serve as a resource, has gone from being an esoteric, academic concept to something that businesses can employ with tangible results.

- **Many-to-Many Customer Support** – Even at this early stage of social media we are seeing consumers answer questions, make application recommendations, share instruction manuals and troubleshoot problems. These interactions are not always accurate or endorsed. Brands in industries like healthcare, finance and insurance will have a difficult time fostering environments that let customers provide service to each other, but in other industries, speed, low cost and authenticity will make social media based customer service extremely attractive.

Is All of This Just Hype?

Some people will say that all of this promise sounds remarkably similar to the Internet Boom and Bust. And we all know how that turned out, right? Actually the Internet is proving to be bigger and more remarkable than almost all of the pundits predicted. Sure, the timing might have been off and some of the outlandish claims never came true, but it is hard to dispute the myriad ways that the Internet has changed everyday life. Social media will be the same.

Kenneth J. Weiss

Chapter 5

Being Social and Getting Down To Business
Social media is not social commerce by default

Social media is an incredible tool for having conversations. Listening. Responding. Sharing. Social media, by nature, is not a perfect venue for selling. Many companies have been enamored with the low cost of entry and have interpreted that as an opportunity to have huge ROAS (Return on Ad Spend.) Social media can help an e-commerce effort by being part of an integrated plan, but for the vast majority of brands it is not a stand alone moneymaker.

Do You Have A Super Model?

Social media exists within the greater context of your business model. Are you a dotcom pure play? Are you a dotcom retailer that carries brands from multiple manufacturers? Are you a manufacturer who primarily sells to retailers but has some direct sales? Are you a catalog/web firm who sells to customers without any retail presence? These are just a few of many models, but it is important to understand how the model fits with the potential for a socially-assisted sale. As you start to employ social media with the idea of increasing sales, you will need to understand what to look for and where. Should the effort create sales on your own dotcom site? Will the effort create sales at a retail partner's brick and mortar stores or dotcom properties? Will you have fast enough access to the data to know? Also, like almost every other marketing activity, direct attribution can be difficult to determine. Even in the online world where technologies allow for click through and view through tracking, there is always some amount of activity that cannot be definitively attributed.

Do Your Customers Even Want This?

Longtime internet pros will remember the days when the masses rebelled against the commercialization of the web. The same holds true for today's social media, and the consequences may be more severe since the people who rebel against you may be your own customers. If you cultivated your social media efforts under the pretense of service and "listening" a sales-oriented message might seem like it's out of left field.

Do You Have A Well-Developed Channel Strategy?

The world of commerce is becoming more multi-channel each day. Products can be purchased on the web, over the phone, in catalogs and in stores. Layered on top of these possibilities are search and web shopping tools that allow people to easily compare prices, read reviews and find similar items. These factors make channel management critical to social media programs intended to increase sales. Channel management as a discipline looks across all of a company's active channels to correctly manage selling opportunities. In some cases this may mean that certain products are only available in a limited number of stores. Sometimes manufacturers develop exclusive SKUs for specific retailers.

34

What Is Your E-Commerce Track Record?

If your company does not have a proven e-commerce track record that includes your own site, comparison engines, paid search, search engine optimization and email, should you really be jumping into social media with the hopes of sell-sell-selling? Probably not. E-commerce is more than just an "add to cart" button. Your organization needs to be fundamentally sound at merchandising, fulfillment, customer service, and all of the other e-commerce basics. If you do not have a solid e-commerce foundation, social media will make your problems worse – it won't make them go away.

You Will Need To Employ Sales Promotion

Social Media by nature likes things that are interesting and different. That's what people talk about. That's what gets traction. Feeding the social space your regular products at their regular prices is only going to be so interesting. Some people will talk about it, but you will not see a gigantic up-tick in sales. This is where sales promotion comes into play. Do a search for social media success stories on Google and you will find dozens of stories about successful social media coupons, special offers, product trials, pricing programs, daily deals and more. All of these are forms of sales promotion. However, sales promotion has never been a "one size fits" all solution. Some brands do not want to condition the marketplace to believe that everyday prices are only imaginary and that a better price is just a sale away. For those companies the price is the price. Other companies may not have the margins or marketing dollars to support a program that the social sphere would find remarkable.

Sales promotion can do a couple of things: It can create a short term burst of interest. This may or may not include a short term sales improvement. It can also bring new users into your space. The best sales promotion programs are those that create a short term burst of sales and have lasting effects on the brand and the market.

Are Your Preaching to the Choir?

Every brand involved in social media is followed by a slightly different composition of users. Some brands have thousands of hardcore followers who receive emails, use features on Facebook, subscribe to updates and more. Others have a more causal fan base who tune in and out without using any social media tools to establish firm connections. In addition to these differences in the composition of the audience, brands have different compositions when it comes to their social media activity. Many brands allow their user base to build naturally and spend most of the time communicating with the people that find them. Other brands spend much more time trying to attract and build a base of constituents in the social space. When you really dig into the numbers, some major brands that move hundreds of thousands of pieces of inventory each week in traditional channels have only a few hundred or a few thousand followers.

If you have a large market share in a sizable market, isn't it silly to have only a few hundred or a few thousand followers?

This small audience problem is worse if you direct a social commerce program against the small base. Yes, current customers are your best prospects, but if you have already maxed out the lifetime customer value for this group, you won't generate any significant incremental business.

Be Great Embedding

Many social media properties are developing extensions and tool kits that allow companies to embed social media experiences directly into their sites. YouTube was a pioneer at this practice when it developed the simple code to allow developers to embed videos into thier sites. Facebook joined this trend when it began to offer the "Like" functionality as an embed for sites.

Social media extensions are tricky. Any traffic you bring to your site is a valuable commodity – it simply should not be "leaked" right back into the web. At the same time however, correctly embedded social media tools will strengthen your value proposition, extend your site deeper into the corners of the web and attract new people.

Remember, your social media plan should include participation on other sites along with social thinking on your own sites.

Where Social Media is Becoming Social Commerce

Each day new social media concepts are coming to market with more and more commerce capabilities. Variations of marketplaces, private sales, auctions, gift experiences and more are reshaping traditional transactions. You will need to have a firm understanding of margin dollars, fulfillment costs, customer acquisition costs, customer churn, lifetime customer value, add-on sales and how new, experimental activities can be included in your larger e-commerce strategy. You also need to understand what these do to your brand and your long-term pricing strategy.

A few examples include:

- **Group Sites** – Group sites come in a variety of different formats but all use the idea of an aggregated number of purchases being used as leverage to lower the price of the item.

- **Social Shopping** – Many new sites combine elements of comparison engines, retail sites, review sites and social networks to create experiences where people shop collaboratively by sharing wish lists, splitting the costs of items and up voting/down voting items.

- **Daily Deal Web Sites** – Sites which feature one killer deal each day have been around for a long time, and these sites are being amped with social tools.

The Line Between Social Media and Social Commerce Is Getting Blurry, But It Is Still There

No doubt as you read this, dozens if not hundreds of companies are making social media work as social commerce. But remember, this is a very small percentage of businesses using the web. Social media will be one of many new areas where a company can stretch its commerce wings. In-store kiosks, online marketplaces, and the mobile space deserve just as much, if not more, attention.

38

Chapter 6

If You Want to Know Social, You've Got to Get Intimate With Mobile
Social media and mobile devices are made for each other

Social is hot and mobile is hot. It is inevitable that they will hook up in big, big ways. Today's world is an always-on, always-connected place. Mobile technology is coming of age at the same time as the Millenials. What a pair! The real strength of mobile is not that it is growing as an island, but rather how it is growing in an open, connected way. Facebook provides daily evidence of this as people use the app to update their pages and interact with friends. Other properties, like Foursquare and Instagram, have quickly developed passionate fans.

A lot is happening in the mobile space. New initiatives are allowing for synchronized sessions across multiple sites and companies are rapidly figuring out how to launch mobile sites and make the "standard" site more mobile friendly. Social experiences are being deeply integrated within devices and several social media properties are working on their own devices. Mainstream device manufacturers are continually releasing phones, tablets, and other mobile devices that are fun, functional and funky.

The relationship between mobile and social is steamy and will only get hotter.

Location Based Data

The ability of phones and networks to determine and communicate a user's location is being used in a number of ways. Even if the data is not being captured in a dynamic way, social experiences are giving users reasons to share their locations. As the number of devices increases, the saturation of users in a particular area will increase as well. The entire cycle will feed itself, and geographic-based elements within social media experiences will grow exponentially.

Personalization Technologies

People use their devices on the go – they are multitasking in unbelievable ways. Any site or experience needs to be relevant almost instantaneously. Fortunately, personalization technology is rapidly evolving. Personalization can use crowd-based wisdom, sophisticated models or predictive technology that leverages recorded individual patterns. Personalization will help bind the mobile and social worlds by creating social experiences that are immediately captivating to the user who has just seconds to glance at their device.

Check Out These Apps, Baby

As funny as it sounds, apps may turn out to be the killer app for mobile devices. Apps come in all flavors: games, news, music, sports, shopping, and, yes, social media. All of these are important because they make consumers more familiar with the process of selecting, downloading and using apps. Apps also increase the time spent using the device and the number and depth of interactions each day. So, while you are reading the reviews for that new car, you might as well tell all of your friends what you are doing.

Facial and Voice Recognition Technology

Want to know the name of that cute girl over there? Ask your phone. The cameras and microphones in phones have the ability to do more than just take pictures and make calls. The camera can be paired with facial recognition technology to find people in crowds, put names with faces and do other things, like sorting through pictures to find out who was at that party you can't quite remember. Voice and audio recognition technology can be used in similar ways to identify voices or to grab snippets of sounds and sync a television, radio or streamed event with content in a social experience.

Low Cost Voice and Data Plans with Improved Speeds

Although cost and speed may seem like different ideas, the two are really one and the same. Low cost with unusable speed is not viable, and high speed at high cost is not attainable by the masses. Increased speeds at lower costs have intersected with another market force: the power of referrals. Even very early in the history of cell phones, companies began to tailor pricing models around groups of families and friends. Don't be surprised to see models in the future that leverage social media and mobile marketing to create monthly plans that are amazingly low priced.

Wearable Computers and Smart Clothing

Funny, when the subject of wearable computers pops up, some people act as though you've been sniffing toner. Wearable computers are all around us! People have swanky Bluetooth headsets hung on their ears, iPods clipped to their belts, watches that are true multi-function computers and

41

not to mention personal GPS units and gadgets like pedometers. Don't forget about medical devices like insulin
pumps, pain management systems and pacemakers. All of
these devices will soon be integrated into the social web.
These devices will communicate where you are, how you
are and what's around you along with a constant stream of
data about all aspects of you.

E-Readers

Steve Jobs famously quipped, "People don't read anymore."
While they may read less of traditional formats, reading is
alive and well. When you study the evolution of e-readers
you will notice that they are changing from connect and
disconnect devices to always connected devices. Soon the
line between tablet computers and e-readers will be indistinguishable and a new era of social reading will arise that
blends writing, publishing, marketing and the actual pur-
chase process into a brand new social, on the go experience.

Getting Social in Cars – Who Needs The Back Seat?

Nothing says "mobile" like America's love of cars, and very
soon people will be moving from the back seat to the front
when they want to connect. Automakers are using hands-
free technology, in-dash flat screens and other design features to integrate social media with vehicles. Not only will
traditional social media activities be brought to the car, but
the entire automobile culture will be reflected back to social
media. Your gas mileage, location, radio station and other
data points will seamlessly stream to the social world. Stuck
in traffic? Why flip people off when you can friend them?

What's Next?

The social and mobile mashup will continue to intensify. Improved analytics will allow companies to measure activities more completely and sharpen their investments to lift key performance metrics. Marketers will be tapping into new types of pay-to-play programs. Venues like move theaters, concert halls and amusement parks will be designed with social media in mind. And, this space will become the home to new visionaries who combine the possibilities in new and remarkable ways.

Chapter 7

What People Do, Why They Do It and How
A look at the different consumer types in social media

Lots of people are doing all kinds of stuff in the social media world. Marketers would like to think that the social media space is filled with loyal consumers having deep, "authentic" discussions about their brands. Well...a little. Social media is filled with all types of people. Some are looking for a good time. Some are looking for trouble. Some are discussing brands and some are dissing them. Don't think that social media is simple and that everyone is on your side.

The Scientific Look

Forrester Research is one of the leaders in the realm of social media research and analysis. Their landmark work on social media identified specific types of users which they tracked on an ongoing basis.

- **Creators – About one quarter of all social media users engage in "creation" activities which include maintaining blogs, creating web pages, writing articles and uploading original music and videos.**

- **Conversationalists – This group represents the large number of social media users who primarily participate by updating their status on social sites. About one third of users fall into this group at some point.**

45

- Critics – This is the group that answers the "was it good for you?" question. Critics post reviews, submit ratings and comment on blogs and content sites. Again, about one-third of users fall into this group at some point.

- Collectors – Approximately 1 in 5 social media users participate in collection activities. Collectors are a group that thrives in the segmentation technologies of social media. They may follow a topic using an RSS feed, vote/promote content or add tags to material.

- Joiners – The more the merrier, right? To be considered a joiner a person most likely has an account at one or more social properties. According to Forrester this is about 60% of social media users.

- Spectators – Like to watch? You are not alone. This is Forrester's largest group. About 70% of social media users do this: read blogs, watch videos, read reviews, etc.

- Inactives – These are the people that joined the party, but don't do much of anything.

No investigation of social media should be done without a review of Forrester's past and current work. Read it all end to end - and often.

Several other types of users and behaviors should be studied. Some will turn you on, and some will turn you off.

Brand Zealots

Brand zealots are those people who forward material, create content and positively comment on a brand. Their motives are not always altruistic. Sometimes they are looking for free products or some other type of spiff. Some, though, are truly maniacal about their favorite brands.

46

The Less Than Fanatical Fan

One measure of success used by companies when evaluating their social media presence is the number of fans (or "likes") they have on Facebook. ExactTarget released some interesting findings in a recent study: "To show my support for the company," was given as a reason 39% of the time as to why people followed brands. However: "To receive discounts and promotions" was the most frequently provided reason at 40%. Other reasons touched on curiosity, recommendations from friends and just for fun. When looking at your audience, think about quality, not just size.

The Grudgers

People with a grudge are as aggressive, if not more aggressive, when it comes to using social media than the people who love your brand. Don't assume that any social media experience you create will be a happy playground where everyone says nice things and minds their manners.

Grudgers have been known to remix content, post contrary opinions, leave negative feedback and to drip-drip-drip ongoing derogatory comments on pages. Social media experiences are not always moderated so the Grudgers can and will get exposure.

People Pretending To Be Other People For Money

Many brands have stated that they want to embrace social media so they can show their true, authentic self to consumers, and then they go and hire PR, advertising and social media firms to run their campaigns. It's true and that's just the way that it is. Whether the "social media" person is an internal or external resource, a manager needs to understand that there are good ones and bad ones. A chubby,

47

over-the-hill marketing guy trying to resurrect his career by saying he "gets" social media probably does not.

Super Users and Influencers

Super Users and Influencers are those individuals who have mastered social media and built large, powerful followings. These types of people are a favorite of marketers because they have both reach and authority. It is commonplace to invite these individuals to events, allow them to test product, include them in ambassador groups and use other tactics to gain their favor.

Short Term Noobs

A Noob (Newbie) is a person who is simply new to the system. In the social media space Noobs tend to find something they like and advance, or they leave quickly not sure what all of the fuss is about. Noobs can also be property specific. A person who is a super user on another property can be a Noob to a new creation. Herein lies the dilemma: Each new property must bring something new and different to the table while relying on proven conventions and time-tested usability techniques to allow for success without frustration.

Oh Master, Masterful Webmaster

Unlike the person who is paid to be someone else, the Masterful Webmasters uses social media to promote a site or sites that they control in order to create revenue. These guys join pay for performance programs (cost-per-lead, cost-per-acquisition, affiliate programs, etc) to create serious amounts of cash. For them social media is a way to tap in to other people's pools of collected traffic. They will post comments, add links, submit articles, upload water marked images, anything, to snatch some traffic and turn it into cash.

The Sloppy Spammer

The Sloppy Spammer can be a wannabe social pro, Grudger or Brand Zealot who just doesn't get it. These people blast away with comments or links just hoping that something will stick.

The Bad Guys

Social media is no different than all other parts of the web. If a person has bad intentions, the open nature and sophisticated tools of social media can be used to do damage.

- **Hot Puppets** – These are carefully cultivated fake personas owned by marketers, spammers and gamers. The imaginary hot guys and girls are designed to get users to try new sites, download apps, become fans, etc. These hot puppets are completely fictional and only exist at the whim of its owner.

- **Embellished Guy/Girl** – Sad but true. Many people are using social media as a way to go on that diet or get that "job" they always wanted. Dozens of stories have been written and even a movie was produced that chronicled guys and girls falling in love with someone over the web only to find out that the person was not who they were lead to believe. (Manti Teo, your table is ready.) Not only is it being done, it is being done poorly. Several people have been busted after they posted a stock image as their pic but failed to edit out the watermark.

- **Pump and Dumpers** – No its not what you think...well maybe it is. "Pump and dump" in the classic sense is falsely promoting a stock to increase its value and selling at the top. Social media and its ability to spread information has been used imaginatively in pump and dump schemes. In some instances fake news stories were created under believable URLs and the link was then forwarded as proof that XYZ company is the next big thing.

- Pedophiles – These sickos have always used the web, and now they are using social media in disturbing ways. Although most sites have policies designed to protect children, pedophiles are using social media to share pictures, links and videos. In some cases they have used social media to share tactics for approaching children. Pedophiles also regularly create false profiles and use those to engage with children. They have been known to use multiple profiles to harvest different bits of information from their targets. So ask yourself, if your teenager has 2,000 friends on Facebook, are they all real people?

- Hackers – Hacking is alive and well on social media sites. Thousands of people have been burned by hackers who have gained access to their accounts and sent erroneous information on their behalf. Sometimes links are sent that lead to bogus stories, or worse, to downloads that contain some form of malware.

Creating Real Satisfaction: The Value of True Customer Insights

Any good marketing program is driven by true customer insight.Why does one ad resonate while another does not? Why does one product fly off the shelf while another heads to the clearance aisle? Customer insight.

In the social space customer insight operates on two levels. First a marketer needs to understand why certain customer segments participate in the social sphere. What is that insight? Are they looking for information? Creating a mental getaway from the grind of their daily life? Are they driven to find solutions to give their children a better life? Next, what insights exist about the customers and your brand within the social space? This is where a well developed brand strategy really comes into play. The actual features and benefits of your product may not be viable in a social media context. What part of the brand is relevant?

Social Soreness

Some users get worn out in the social space. They hit it hard and then decide it is just not worth it. Dozens of celebrities, athletes and entertainers have abandoned their popular Twitter accounts because they could not find satisfaction or value. Blogs are another prime example. If you search the web for blogs on any topic you will easily find hundreds. Exciting right? Dig a little deeper and you will start to notice that many have been abandoned - the last post was months or years ago. The same is true for videos. Check out some random videos and YouTube and check the date of the last comment. Could be months ago. Social media is growing rapidly, but there is a massive amount of churn at play, too.

Remember, It's Social Media, Not Commercial Media

For many people social media space is perceived as a place for truly social interaction. As users, they are not interested in advertising, thinly veiled PR or marketing stunts. Some brands have created undercover campaigns that are so undercover that they were never able to close the loop and connect the activity with the brand. Ongoing research shows that even people who have friended a brand are not receptive to marketing overtures.

51

Users like it certain ways. Make sure you understand them
before you get too frisky with social media.

Chapter 8

Take Your Time
You can't hurry your way through social media

Having a good, let alone great, social media program requires time. "Our current staff can handle it," is the second greatest social media fib right behind, "we can do it without a budget."

The hard fact is that your existing staff does not have the time.

Most businesses focus on content creation which takes time and talent. What they fail to recognize is that other essential activities are time eaters as well. In fact, these may take more time than the creation of content.

Creating A Reasonable Name Strategy

Nothing, absolutely nothing, will get a marketer in more hot water than the boss-man reading an article about the "hot new social media site" and finding out that somebody else has already registered the brand name as a user name. How many of these new sites should you check? 5? 10? 20? Twenty might be a good start, and unless you are way ahead of the curve, your brands have already been snatched up. So what is the strategy for a consistent, on-brand name scheme in the social media space? Even if you use name discovery tools, this is an answer that will require some serious research and thinking.

Reading, Researching and Responding

When the boss comes into your office and says "Did you see what that person wrote on our wall?" you'd better know. Reading comments (moderating when possible), checking reviews, watching posts, keeping track of the discussion in all of its forms can take hours. f you are responsible for multiple brands the task is that much harder.

That is just part one.

Next you will need to figure out what is going on. If a person complains about a problem in the instruction manual, you will need to find one and see what they are talking about. If they are complaining about a late order, you will need to track down the order number and do some homework. If the person claims that your product did not work, it's time for damage control.

After that you will need to figure out how to respond. You will need to get input from brand, product and legal teams. Depending upon the visibility of the content you may need to get senior management's approval.

And then? Repeat. Repeat. Repeat.

Monitoring, Measuring and Crunching the Numbers

Nobody wants to read through hundreds of comments or posts to see "how the campaign is doing." Social media monitoring tools are becoming quite sophisticated and are bringing quantitative data to the party. As you look across efforts, analyze campaign effects and integrate other types of data such as paid search spending, email marketing and other digital tactics, you will need to spend time turning the data into information.

Promotions Management

Most brands use promotions extensively in social media campaigns. Contests can require considerable planning, cooperation from legal, winner selection, notification, and more. Even simple promotions using coupon codes will require support. Consumers will call customer service with questions. Some will be easy and some will not. Correctly managed promotions can create good will. Poorly run promotions are nothing but buzz kill.

Sales, Marketing and Supply Chain Integration

Which products will the company be banking on to be hot sellers? Which items are still in stock? What happens if a particular promotion is a runaway hit? Will you be able to keep the item in stock? Social media efforts can not be run in a vacuum. Even if the stated goal is to promote the "brand" and not individual products, a product discussion is inevitable.

Channel Integration

Retailers can be persuaded to add lines, carry more inventory and give better placement to products if they understand the level of marketing support an item or line will receive. In the past, substantial TV buys were used as leverage to improve retail sell in. Now retailers are curious as to what social media efforts will be in place. Social media professionals will need to know how to present the work, not just how to do the work. As a company makes its channel strategy more multifaceted, the social media strategy will need to be more complex as well.

55

Watching The Competition

Chances are your competitors are trying new things. Keeping track of the competition can be very time consuming, and it can be incredibly valuable. If they just launched a new product, what are people saying? How is that new feature being received? Did their latest promotions cause a ripple on the deal boards? Can you determine how much product they may have moved? Valuable information! And, time consuming, too!

Keeping Up To Speed with New Opportunities

New social media possibilities and strategies continue to emerge. There are new sites and systems to hook up with every day. How will your company keep track of the possibilities? Where does investigation and exploration cross the border into "goofing off." How will HR and IT be able to tell the difference? Give a person the green light to spend unlimited time online and guess what? They will!

Legal Follow Up

This time killer is not even fun: following up on legal issues. Legal matters can be miserable because doing something or failing to do something can sometimes be considered setting a precedent. So, blowing something off is not an option. You'll need to make friends with your legal department and you may learn more legalese than you ever wanted to know.

Exhausted Yet?

Social media requires time. Lots of time. You can cut corners, but you will always get out what you put in.

Chapter 9

If You Are Not Ready to Listen and React, You Are Not Ready

You will need to service your campaign, not just blabber

Ears are a big turn on. The social media crowd knows if you hear their whispers. They know if screams are being ignored. Listening gets things going. Listening goes beyond simply browsing comments, reviews and posts. Being ready to listen means being ready to react, being ready to confront painful information and being ready to respond in a fair and complete manner. And, remember, all of this will happen in a very public way. These are not under-the-sheets conversations. Social media listening is public exhibitionism in its barest, biggest state.

Get Ready For Bad News

Companies hope for good news, such as positive comments, and are quick to dream about what they will do with them. However many are not willing to consider that the overriding sentiment could be negative. This is very similar to traditional crisis management planning where companies think it is a necessity but not needed if "we stay out of trouble."

Social media is different because a lone, dissenting voice can impact hundreds, if not thousands, of people. Social media listening needs to be built around these types of exceptions.

The community will quickly recognize if only the positive thoughts and feelings are being heard. Policies need to be established that give negative comments higher priority than positive ones.

Allocated Resources

How many hours a week have you budgeted for social media resources? Have a number? Now, how much of that has been earmarked for strategy, asset creation and posting, versus monitoring and interaction? Many social media initiatives fail because they are budgeted as old-style, one-way, delivery campaigns and not two-way interactions.

Becoming Systems Ready

Social media is viewed as a "lower cost" way to market and build brands. While this may be true, "lower" does not mean free. Being ready to listen means having systems in place.

- **Social Media Monitoring Tools - Social media monitoring tools make it easy to statistically track share of voice as well as sentiment. Brands can identify power advocates, detractors and more. These are essential for benchmarking and tracking the progress of social media campaigns.**

- **CRM Tools - While CRM is an accepted part of customer service, marketing and operations, it has not been embraced as an essential part of social media. Yet. Customers will continue to move their gripes and questions from email and 800 numbers to the social media space. If the emails and calls have been rigorously logged in the past, why not the social media conversation in the future?**

- **FAQs and Knowledge Bases - Part of being a good listener is responding quickly. Knowledge management tools in-**

cluding system-accessible FAQs and knowledge bases are essential. Social media teams must be easily able to find answers while being confident that the information is accurate and up to date.

- Approved Scripting - Often the same comments, questions, criticisms and complaints will arise repeatedly. Responding consistently is important. Consumers will latch on to small differences in wording and try to assemble conspiracies. Approved scripting ensures that the company's response is consistent and on-brand.

- Defined Work Flows - Who needs to be in the loop, when, about what? Figuring this out on the fly can work, but it will slow down the process. Being good means being responsive. Defined work flows are invaluable.

So What Is Good Listening?

So how do you tell if you are doing it right? Here are some tips:

- Demonstrate that you Understand the Question - This is where the one-size fits all response is deadly. Imagine the following post. "Help! My husband's birthday is tomorrow and the 800 line is going to voicemail. I'm trying to put together his new gas grill and the supply line does not seem to fit on the burner assembly."
Response: "<name>, thank you for purchasing one of our products. Customer service reps are available Mon - Fri 8 - 6 EST." Did the response make things better or worse?

- Set Expectations for Follow Up - When is the last time consumer wrote a good, old-fashioned paper letter to your company? Sure, it still happens, but not often. When it was popular, mail, as the device, carried certain expectations of response time. A reply in WEEKS was probably acceptable. Phone and email have greatly contracted those expectations. Social media goes one step further. The expectation is immediacy. Responses and interactions should convey details about the type and timing of follow-up. Be careful with the wording! It will be taken as a promise.

- **Stay In Touch During Delays - When delays in a response become inevitable, keep the consumer informed.**

Who You Are Listening To Can Skew Your Data

Listening to certain people and listening in certain places can greatly color (or discolor) your interpretation of the social media discussion. For instance your Facebook page may have both positive and negative comments, but since it is populated with fans the conversation will generally be positive. Now, go read the comments about your products on a retailer's web site. This is neutral ground. The overall tone of the conversation may be much more negative. Blogs, video channels, communities, discussion boards and review sites are likely to each have their own vibe.

When Things Go Unexpectedly Well

Enjoy it. It won't last forever.

When Things Go Unexpectedly Bad

It will last a while and feel like forever.

Chapter 10

"Going Viral" Is Not A Strategy
Runaway hits are nice, but not guaranteed

If any part of your social media plan hinges on the phrase "go viral," you don't have much of a plan.

As some background: "Going viral" is the new Holy Grail for marketers. The hope is that your staff or agency will create something that is so funny, compelling, gross, cool, awesome, hideous, offensive, etc. etc. that it will be passed along and seen million and millions of times.

Let's be clear. That has happened and is happening. Dozens of web sites track the viral superstars of the week. Some videos go viral and rack up millions of views. No denying it: that's powerful. But what you don't notice are the thousands of videos and social media programs that go nowhere.

Many companies are sold on obscenely large budgets, questionable tactics, off-color content and other shady stuff under the premise that these methods will make something go viral.

Odds are "going viral" won't happen.

What Can Go Viral?

Lots of stuff. Entire campaigns, emails, promotions, coupon codes, images, videos, stories, jokes, pranks, songs - you name it.

Can You Predict What Will Go Viral?

Nope. You can easily look at all of the videos, pictures and other memes that have racked up millions of views or impressions and find commonalities, but replicating those commonalities does not guarantee success. Many of those viral successes also lack one critical element: a commercial message. Many of the top videos are quirks of life that resonated with users. No attempt was being made to push a brand or product. Gatorade beat the odds (kinda) with the famous "Ball Girl" clip. In the video, a ball girl at a minor league baseball stadium makes an unbelievable catch of a foul ball. After the catch she trots back to her folding chair and takes a sip of her favorite sports drink. No logo. No tagline. Nothing. The clip went viral because people thought it was real. Not because they thought it was an advertisement worth passing along. Only after it was a hit, did Gatorade step forward. Ironically the ad agency that produced the clip had already parted ways with Gatorade by the time the video hit the big time.

Social, Interactive and Viral – What's the Dif?

Sometimes these terms are used interchangeably. Viral refers to a video, coupon, campaign or other element being passed along repeatedly. Interactive simply means that the user can play or contribute. Social means that the experience itself changes or grows stronger by nature of the group's interaction.

62

Does Viral Mean Free?

People think viral means free, but the reality is that many brands invest some serious cash into attempting to kick start a viral effort.

- **Ideas and Finished Elements Aren't Cheap -** Many successful viral instances are the product of beating the odds with lots of attempts. Volkswagen created a series of videos showing ways the brand could make life quicker as part of the Fast Lane campaign. Most of the videos garnered a reasonable number of views, but only one went viral. Many brands create multi-part campaigns hoping that they will strike gold with one of the components. The successes of bands, comedians, film makers, cartoonists and regular brands are proof that you have to continually deliver ideas in order to come up with something that will go viral.

- **Big Production Budgets, Tons of Time, Sometimes Both -** One genre of videos that regularly goes viral-level views is flash mobs. Flash mobs are heavily orchestrated events where dozens, or even hundreds, of people simultaneously break into a song, dance or theatrical performance. Flash mobs have turned up in train stations, city streets, parks, stores and even at an outdoor taping of the Oprah Winfrey show. Some groups like Improv Everywhere have made these signature events, while other brands like T-Mobile stage the events and only claim ownership afterwards. The events are a joy to watch because they appear so spontaneous and unrehearsed. In reality they are planned for weeks and require the involvement of huge casts (not cheap.) Contrast these with the viral hits of the music duo Pomplamoose. Their videos feature singer Nataly Dawn and musician Jack Conte in a small apartment crammed with patchwork recording equipment and wonderfully whimsical musical instruments. Big budget? No.

Huge time investment? You betcha. The end product: absolutely entrancing. Their covers of tunes like Lady Gaga's "Telephone" and Beyonce's "Single Ladies" have racked up millions of views and the couple capitalized on their YouTube stardom by landing a feature gig on a Hyundai Campaign. Probably the most famous low budget viral wonder was the OK Go video for their single, "Here It Goes Again." The premise: The little known band had very little money, a video camera and a few old exercise treadmills. The rest is history.

- A Seeding Effort - Many companies attempt to kick start the viral effort by launching a program within their existing social network. Using a few dozen people or a few hundred people in an attempt to create a nuclear chain reaction of awareness is referred to as Little Seed Marketing. If you want to be serious, you need Big Seed Marketing. Big Seed Marketing is essentially paying for an initial blast of awareness in hopes that it will start the viral domino effect. The seeds can take multiple forms. Some companies aggressively hunt down opinion leaders in the space and ask them to blog, tweet or comment on the campaign. Sites like Digg and Reddit actually offer paid advertising positions that are nearly indistinguishable from user supplied content. Some ad formats allow for a YouTube embedded video player that allows the video to be distributed across vast advertising networks while racking up views that can catapult the video on to the coveted "Most Viewed" list. Even the wildly successful Old Spice "The Man Your Man Could Smell Like Campaign" used a Super Bowl commercial to get the party started. (Not cheap.) Small efforts may require paying for placement on the home page of a target-appropriate site.

- Adding a Social Imperative Using Cause Marketing - Cause marketing is a great way to fuel social interaction. Cause marketing can take various forms: making a dona-

64

tion, sponsoring a charity, providing product, etc. These efforts attend to attract like-mined people just the way social media does. By tapping into a community and supporting a cause that fits their point of view, brands are able to create a win-win relationship. These efforts may be cheaper than pure advertising plays, but still not free.

- **Freebies, Samples and Promotions** - Nothing creates buzz like "Free." Offering free or discounted product is a quick way to get people to spread the word. However, this is not always the best tactic for the brand.

Experts Can Be Helpful

A number of firms and individuals are establishing themselves as viral experts. Some are cheap, some are not, but they can be very helpful in creating big picture strategies and tweaking the nuances like titles, headlines, screen grabs and images. Caution: Hire at you own risk, and be prepared for failures.

Who's Beat The Odds and Gone Viral

Viral success are out there, but you'll need to study them to determine if they were commercial or non-commercial in nature.

- **The Lucky Brands** - BlendTec, Sony Bravia, Soulja Boy Smirnoff, Gatorade, T-Mobile, Chik-Fil-A, Starbucks, Dollar Shave Club and others have had viral hits, each with a different level of brand delivery.

Cool Stuff. No Purchase Required

Many of the legendary viral hits had no commercial message. They were just charming or embarrassing events that people liked to share including Charlie Bit My Finger, David Goes to The Dentist, Miss Teen South Carolina, Philippine Prison Dancing, Dramatic Prairie Dog, Leave Brittney Alone, Bed Intruder. These lead people to burn billions of hours of what could have been productive time.

Chapter 11

Metrics Are Slippery
Measurements may not be clear, but you owe yourself metrics

Social media is like a great Friday night party. Lots of conversation. Lots of people "liking." Some pictures of family being shared. Topics of every nature being discussed. Brands making small appearances. Music. Phones. Games. People making friends. People making friends with benefits.

Now imagine this specific party happening in a few different apartments in a building. Now imagine that building being repeated in a complex. Now imagine multiple complexes in a city. Now image multiple cities. Now imagine...you get the point.

This little analogy tells quite a bit about social media and the challenges of measuring it. Social media is incredibly decentralized with pockets of conversation happening everywhere. Some conversations waterfall from each other while others overlap. Some conversations happening in the same place, actually have nothing to do with what other people are talking about. Information is shared. Sometimes reciprocated. Sometimes not. People respect different people. People like different people. And in this age of connectivity, the conversation quickly leaps across venues to other groups of people. There is some order within this cacophony, but beware: the metrics are slippery.

Friends With Features & Benefits – A Marketer's Guide to Scoring with Social Media

Everyone's Yardstick is Different

Social media metrics is an emerging field with a number of great companies. However, in their quest to differentiate their offering, many social media metrics firms have developed their own specific methodologies for measurement. As a result two different companies may use the same words for a metric, but use different methodologies for collecting and presenting the data. Don't assume that you can compare reports from two different sources and identify changes or trends.

Metrics Change Between Properties

Traditionally web metrics could be used to compare and understand web sites. Two retail web sites could be compared using their conversion rates. Two independent bands could be evaluated based upon the number of downloads. Two web sites for leading consumer brands could be compared using the number of visitors, page views or the average time on the site. Social media is a bit different. The nature of the experience from site to site, app to app, or property to property is different.

Facebook and Flickr might share some common DNA as "web sites," but the fundamental user experience for each is very different. You need to develop an understanding of the metrics within each.

- **Data is going to be relative to your level of involvement. User activity will change based upon the quality and frequency of your participation.**

- **The overall size of the property will shape your metrics. For example, lots of photo sharing sites exist, but they have dramatically differing user bases. Having an equal**

68

number of views on two sites is not necessarily equivalent.

- Social sites vary in their level of connectivity to other sites and the general Internet. A video view might be counted if it takes place on the hosting site and a view could also be counted if a person embedded the video on a different site using the embed link from the hosting site.

- The level of participation by your competitors will change the metrics. You may have a 100% share of voice within a small social experience, but that level of participation would only constitute 20% within a more active experience.

- The authority of a site within a sphere will shape metrics. Imagine two bloggers engaging in a comment discussion with readers. One blog is extremely well read and respected within your industry while the other is tangentially relevant at best. Even if both conversation streams are vibrant and substantive, they are not equal.

Comparing Social Media to Other Media

The idea of comparing media and marketing activities is not new. In the world of public relations, quantifying campaign results is done using a variety of methods including Advertising Value Equivalent or Earned Advertising Value. These systems look at the amount of impressions or space captured and create a value based upon equivalent advertising rates. The same can be done with Social Media, but it is not bulletproof. For instance, a consumer might post a picture of a family happily enjoying your product, but in the background might be a competitive product. This would never happen with a traditional advertisement, but it is common in social media. Consumers might also spoof your product or create a satirical piece. Exposure? Yes. Value? Hmm, no. The tenor or voice might also play a role. While an endorsement from a consumer infers objectivity, that consumer's personality or background may taint the recommendation.

Number of Followers and Number Participating

As social media becomes more prevalent and the tools for liking and following brands become ubiquitous, companies will need to sort through their total audience versus the total participating audience. For example, you may have 100,000 fans on a Facebook page, but how many of them interact to any degree? You may have developed an app that was downloaded 50,000 times but can you determine if 50,000 people are actually using it? While in the past, the reach of the experience was considered the most important metric, the true level of participation will be the key metric moving forward.

Visits/Interactions/Usage Instances

This metric is the counterpart to your total audience. It quantifies the amount of use, not the size of the audience. Some social experiences can be measured by visits alone. Some are best measured by the quantity of the interaction. Games, apps and other social experiences need to be measured by the unique number of usage instances.

Duration

For social experiences like apps, measuring the engagement time of users can be useful. If, for example, you have an app-based game, what was the aggregate time spent playing the game by all users? This thinking provides a starting

70

point for looking at average time per user, the number of sessions shorter (or longer) than a particular benchmark, the number of very short abandons, etc.

Frequency

Any particular social experience can be viewed by how often it is used. Conversely, individual users can be examined by their frequency of usage as well. Patterns, seasonality and cyclicality become important.

Depth

Depth metrics change from experience to experience. If you build a social contest, depth metrics will tell you how fully immersed the audience is in the experience. Did they simply sign up? Or did they actively recruit friends? If you developed a game with multiple levels, how many people dabbled, and how many became hardcore? If you developed an app, how many people use the basic functionality and how many people use every feature?

Share of Voice

In any particular part of the social landscape, many brands and entities may be active. Even if you think you are doing a great job, you may be drowned out by someone who is doing an even better job. You will need to understand your share of voice.

Sentiment

Having your brand discussed in the social world is thought to be a desirable activity, but what are people saying? Is it good? Bad? Sentiment scores help quantify the general tonality of the conversation. This can be matched with other mining tools that focus on a particular topic or product.

71

Viral Performance and Pass Along

A number of different tools attempt to capture the great white whale of social media: going viral. In simplest terms, these tools measure the echo or ripple created by people passing along content and links, or at least discussing a particular topic.

ROI Metrics

Social media is where the web itself was 15 years ago; it's in the honeymoon phase. Everyone is happy and in many places, social media is getting the free pass. Those days are coming to an end. While many companies will have the patience to take a longer view of slow shifts in brand metrics, many will want to know what they are getting for the staff, content, agencies and technologies in which they've invested. ROI will vary by brand, but it is in your best interest to lead the development of an ROI model before one is thrust upon you.

Social Media As Referring Traffic

The measurement of social media traffic flowing to web sites, phone and email systems is the most basic form of ROI measurement. Companies that understand acquisition costs, can easily monetize the value of social media traffic.

Cost Per Participant AKA Cost Per Unique Visitor

This metric can be deadly in these experimental days of social media. Pick a social media project and divide the total cost by the total number of people who visited the experience or used it. What is that cost per participant? Now ask yourself could you have generated more impact by using those dollars in a different way? So if you spent $100,000 for a game that 10,000 people played, what type of direct mail piece could you have put together for $10 per name? How much better off would you be had you offered a $10 rebate to 10,000 customers?

Social Media Driven Leads

Social media traffic can not always be connected to sales in the same way that other data can like a house email address file. A carefully cultivated and appended email list or mailing list often can be used in very predictive and scalable sales models. Simply put, companies know what result they will get from an investment in list growth. Sophisticated merge and de-duplication methodologies will evolve to help understand how social media participants become viable customers and at what cost.

Understanding a User

Social media sites and experiences collect an amazing amount of data about their users. Sometimes the user knows. Sometimes they don't. In some cases users find out the hard way how the data is being shared and used. Here are just a few of the data points which can be tied to a user:

- **Demographics - All of the typical stuff.**

- **Expertise - This becomes more important as credibility and authority build in social value.**

- **Influence - Influence can be determined by looking at the number of followers, connections and how often a person's content is passed along.**

- Activity/Recency - To what degree was a person active in a particular social space and when was their most recent activity?

- Sentiment on Topic - You can also drill into a user's sentiment on any particular topic.

If Metrics Are So Slippery, Why Measure?

Social media measurement is not yet an exact, universally standardized science. Getting close, but not there yet. Do not be dissuaded. It is still something worth pursuing.

Benchmark - Yes, it may be difficult to sort through the noise and rapid industry changes may blur the actual results you've affected, but benchmarking still provides a starting point for your analysis.

Measure Impact on Brand Metrics - Simple pre and post tests can determine if your social media activities are moving brand metrics.

Determine Resource Needs - As measurement data is recorded it can be used to create scalable models. If the time and resources expended to create and manage social programs are captured, this along with measurement data, can be used to determine future resource needs.

Track Shift in Business Processes - Social media is seen as a way to reduce media spending, customer service expenditures, PR efforts and CRM programs. The validity of this thinking can only be tested if the right measurements are made.

74

Most Importantly, Create Accountability - Social media can no longer have a free pass. Basic measurement, consistent reporting and transparency create accountability.

Be Your Toughest Critic

If you don't measure, someone else will. Be rigorous. Be consistent. Be honest. Also, be careful about overstating cost savings. Some companies believe that they reduce customer service expenses, but they fail to account for the overall investment in social media. You will typically lose when you swap one customer service rep for a social media specialist.

76

Chapter 12

The Social Media and CRM Hook Up

Your social media strategy will need to work with your CRM strategy

Social media not only holds great promise for brand building, but social media may also become an integral part of a great operations tool as well. "Social CRM" (Social Customer Relationship Management) is part technology, part philosophy, part methodology and part wild-ass-guess. What is certain, though, is that customers have changed. They are more social. And, if a business is to be more social, many parts of the business need to be more social. Marketing will need to get close with customer service, research and operations like never before, so they can all be closer to the customer.

Consumers Want Knowledge. Who Has It?

In many of our lifetimes, the person at the counter - where the product was sold - was the AUTHORITY on using the product. How often is this true today? Big box retailers are continually training their employees, but even the best employees have a hard time keeping up with the ever-changing product offering. As the western economy has matured, the complexity of products and services has outpaced the distribution channel in many cases. Ultra efficient distribution has pushed the task of customer contact back up the distribution chain to the manufacturer. Subject matter experts are required, and that SME often resides high up in the channel. Companies are realizing that they must provide a product or service AND a great customer experience.

The Changing Nature of Conversations

CRM stems from a need to have a single, centralized, measurable and knowledgeable view of customer conversations. In theory, every aspect of a customer interaction should be captured, stored and made accessible to each person in the organization. Traditional conversation streams include:

- **Warranty Cards**

- **Survey Cards**

- **Inbound Phone Calls**

- **Inbound Letters**

- **Inbound Emails**

- **Registrations for Loyalty and Other Programs**

Nudging comfortably up against these conversations are all of the bits and pieces of interactions that take place during the sales process. Lead management and sales CRM manage the interactions for prospects and customers.

Traditional conversations share a critical bit of DNA: the conversation was WITH the company or brand. Social CRM attempts to harness the power of conversations ABOUT the company or brand even if it was not a participant. New conversation streams include:

- **Blog posts**

Kenneth J. Weiss

- Comments

- Wall posts

- Tweets

- Message board posts

- Reviews

- Content interactions

All of these buckets of conversation are critical, and can be identified, measured and influenced.

Understanding Social Conversations

Traditional CRM created robust taxonomies to understand the customer interaction. Customers' actions were categorized with terms like "warranty claim," "performance complaint," "catalog request," etc. Those were fine. Those were accurate. Those were the things done by traditional customers. The social customer does new and different things:

- Downloads a whitepaper

- Views a photo

- Provides content

- Uses a promo code or unlock code

- Starts, and maybe, completes an action

- Updates an account

- Submits a question or comment

- Vents or rants

- Attempts to use social pressure against a company or brand

How You Think of The C Is Critical

To wrap your head around the coming age of Social CRM you need to rethink the C.

The CRM Customer = A person who has purchased a product that has reached back to the company - made a call, sent in a warranty card, sent an email.

The SCRM Customer = A person who has bought the product (or maybe not) and is propelling it in the social world. They may be talking about it to a third party, or they may be interacting within social media with the company that produced or sold it.

CRM conversations primarily affect the relationships between the customer and the company. SCRM conversations affect the relationship of many customers with the brand.

Tackling relationships with people who have not yet even purchased your product may seem intimidating, but the necessity is the reality.

SCRM Becomes More Important As Companies Become More Multichannel

Past relationships with customers were grounded in customer service: companies wanted to have a relationship with individual customers in order to provide outstanding customer service. Now, companies are becoming more multichannel, and having a relationship is a critical part of driving future sales. This can be driving sales at a retailer or driving direct-to-consumer sales.

SCRM Will Provide Enterprise-wide Value

At the heart of SCRM is the belief that the customer experience is valuable to all parts of an organization. SCRM will help detect quality problems early on, identify sales and service issues, and even lead to substantive improvements in future products. In order to succeed, SCRM should not be owned and driven by one part of an organization but shared with all.

82

Chapter 13

You Are Not On Top
Some functionality and policies are beyond your control

What happens in Vegas may stay in Vegas, but what happens in Social Media isn't staying anywhere. A typical user may think they are on top of how data about them is being used. Not even close. Why? The average web user tends to think of their web and mobile usage as a series of discrete events: "I used a search engine." "I updated my Facebook page." "I did some shopping." "I checked my email." What they don't realize, however, is that a vast layer of tracking, modeling and information sharing is going on behind the scenes. These activities are connected. What happens, how it happens and why it happens is governed by individual sites, properties and networks.

Lots of room exists between what is possible and what is illegal.

Users and brands are at the mercy of their policies, and social media ups the stakes of this connected game. Social media is a natural ecosystem for divulging everything. When this is done and connected to all of a person's other activities, the marketing possibilities are mind blowing. A brand may have a presence on a social site, but what the brand will do with the user's data is not the same as what the site might do. The site is the driver's seat.

Social Media Properties Are Rapidly, uh, "Evolving" Their Policies

Social media is a fun business, but it is a business. At the end of the day social media properties need to determine a way to create a valuable, saleable service so they can monetize their social media experience. For these properties, the mountain of behavioral data about their users is an incredible temptation. This data can be used as the kernel for incredible advertising and marketing systems. In some instances, the site may find a use for the data that was not "exactly" covered in the original terms and conditions. What is a site to do? Hmmm. How about change their policies! Facebook has had a few notorious bumps along the way. Facebook users have had experiences of information being shared about them and being shared with them in ways that were shocking. Users were forced to determine the best way to undo the policies changes.

Who Is Sharing Who With Who?

Policy changes might be digestible if they occurred within the context of one site or experience, but social media is after all a sharing environment. Some users cannot even master how to have "private" conversations. Now sites are sharing with each other. Linkedin and Twitter share information in a number of different ways. Think of your own accounts. Are you 100% certain of what is being shared? How did you change your settings? Could you change them back if needed?

Guilt By Association

Companies and brands love the marketing and communications possibilities of social media. However, when a social site changes its policies, a brand can be caught with its pants down and not in a good way. A brand's participation in a marketing or data sharing program may be seen as an endorsement of the systems or polices. In fact, a company might be benefiting from a program that uses data sharing techniques that they do not know about. And maybe even not approve.

As social sites continue to enhance their marketing and data products as a way to monetize traffic, what they reveal about their tactics and methodologies may be kept hidden as part of sound IP protection. A brand may not really know what is happening or what might happen.

Companies also need to take a hard look at the security of social data. The FTC found what they called "serious lapses" in the data security practices of Twitter after hackers breached accounts of a number of users. Anyone important? Yeah, just the President of the United States of America. Twitter agreed to conduct security audits for the next decade.

Consumers Can Tell When Something Is Up

Consumers have a knack for sensing that they or their data is being used. Retargeting, dynamic messaging and specific offers are not always subtle. Consumers know when their actions are being fed to marketers, and these same consumers will also warn other consumers. Ironically, a large number of Facebook posts which tell consumers how to change setting on their accounts appear every time Facebook makes a change to their policies.

Who's Got An Ax to Grind?

Remember, your "fans" will not be the only people using your social media presence. Current and past employees, suppliers, and vendors may all have a different motivation for "using" your social media presence. Fraud, malice and spite will cause all sorts of activities, including trying to out you for questionable practices.

The Tip Of A Very Large Iceberg

Data sharing and behavioral modeling are advancing at an incredibly fast pace. Now imagine what happens when geo-location data collected by mobile devices is added to the mix. Next imagine what happens when facial recognition technology is stirred in. How about the millions of online photos that will be dissected to determine who has been where and who they have been with? After that, add in the connection of data across devices. Even the bundling of Internet, TV and phone services lays the groundwork for the connection of data points across all of those platforms. Companies and brands will decide how tightly they can be tied to "big brother." Brand hubris may foster a feeling of dominance, but big data will wear the pants in that relation-ship.

Chapter 14

Lies, A Little Truth & Transparency

Social media has an incredible way of revealing the unwashed truth

Social media has a knack for exposing lies. Big ones. Little ones. Things that brands have done. Things that brands say they will never do. The argument can be made that "never lying" is therefore the best policy. Probably so. But what about those instances where a brand can be more forthright and more proactive? This openness is what the corporate world refers to as "transparency."

Let's face it. You are already losing the battle of trust. Recent surveys show that people trust word-of-mouth and editorial content far more than advertising. Transparency within your social media program may be your only shot.

For some companies, transparency is a part of the culture. This can be transparency within the walls of the organization, a high level of transparency with customers or both. Social media creates an environment where understanding transparency and the consequences of not being transparent are critical.

Here are a few examples of social media catching people in the act:

- **Pictures of a "green" company employee driving a gas guzzler are published online.**

87

- The (outrageous) executive compensation list of a company claiming to be a "blue collar" firm is leaked through social media.

- Stories about vendors and suppliers of an organic foods company are posted on a Facebook page.

- A music of video of "10 Things to Hate" about a particular company goes viral, and all ten of the points are made easy to research online.

- A cell phone video of a company holiday party is posted showing the employees acting in a way that does not reflect well on the brand.

- A series of customer posts outline the differences between a company's products, price points and distribution points which completely destroys the company's channel management strategy.

- The political affiliations and campaign contributions of a company's board of directors is released online.

Let's Be Real, Transparency Has Its Limits

Lack of transparency is a critical part of almost every business. (In a good way!) Some things are not good candidates for transparency:

- Manufacturing techniques and product formulations

- Product road maps

- Staffing strategies

- Merger and acquisition plans

Secrecy has been used to build brand value, make moves in the marketplace and create operational advantages. This won't change, but in today's social media powered world companies will need to be more open and receptive. Consumers will know when companies are faking it.

A Simple Transparency Yardstick

Here's a simple way to evaluate whether you're big enough when it comes to transparency.

Can what a customer wants to know be known by the customer?

The first part of wrapping your head around this yardstick is thinking like a customer. Not like a single customer, but within the singularity of each customer:

"My child has a wheat allergy. Can they use this product?"

"I believe in buying American-made products. Where is this product made?"

"I like buying from companies that are family friendly. What is it like to work there?"

"I spend my money wisely. Will this product continue to be supported?"

Customers certainly want the answers to easy questions, and they want the answers to hard questions, too. The hard questions are where tough transparency decisions start.

The second part of understanding this message, is grasping the nuances of "can." Not "can" in terms of "are you technically able?" but "can" in terms of "are you willing?'

Are you willing to make the information known? Are you willing to invest in the information, systems, processes, and documents to facilitate its sharing? Are you willing to empower the organization to be transparent?

The Fundamentals of Being Transparent

It's Time to Live Your Brand - Brands must be pointed outward and inward. And, more deeply inward than ever before. This is called living the brand and being authentic.

It's Time To Connect the Silos - If your business has supported internal silos, you are in trouble. Social media will readily expose the dissonance in your organization. If you think the silos are gone – you'd better be sure.

Subject Matter Expertise Is More Important and Fragile Than Ever Before - Business is on the edge of an abyss. For some companies, external experts including brand enthusiasts, industry professionals and journalists are more knowledgeable about products than internal subject matter experts. Job transience, downsizing, retirement and other factors have lead to an incredible amount of lost institutional knowledge. Customers helping other customers may provide a cost savings, but it can be embarrassing.

Understand That The Line Between Professional Lives and Private Lives Is REALLY Blurry - Cell phones and email accessibility have made many positions 24-hour endeavors. Smart phones, connectivity and social media blend

90

work and life even more. You will need to come to grips with how employees blend personal and professional lives – and some of the areas will be very gray. What happens if an employee comments on a company post after hours, at home, from their own computer, is that allowed? If they say something less than glowing? If they do it in a way that is less than ideal? What about if an employee is given permission to engage in social media activities on the job and then leaves the company, who gets the followers?

Do You Understand FTC regulations?

The FTC has jumped into the fray to provide some consumer protection and clarity around blogging. Blogs must now provide some level of disclosure around certain types of activities. Blogs will fulfill these obligations with statements like "Given a review copy" or "paid post – cash or other compensation." Aside from the FTC, publicly traded companies and legally sensitive industries such as banking and healthcare will need to address other regulatory and privacy requirements.

Somebody Is Always Watching

Your fans and friends are watching. Your enemies are watching. The higher the loyalty, the greater the potential for a feeling of betrayal. And negative minded people are looking for a fight. You will need to let it all hang out. Be transparent.

92

Chapter 15

Social Media Gets Nasty
Social media can do exactly what you don't want

Be careful who you connect with. Even customers who LOVE you can turn against you. And those consumers who are just on the edge of your radar? Watch out: they can get downright nasty. Ironically, the things that make social media so alluring: openness, connectivity, and sharing, are the things that can be used against you. Social media programs have gone bad and will continue to go bad.

Typical Ways That Social Media Goes Bad

Social media is evolving so quickly that new ways to screw it up and screw with it are being invented each day. Social damage falls into three main categories:

- **Your own programs turned against you.**

- **Social media tools being used against you.**

- **Self-inflicted damage due to speed, stupidity and negligence.**

All three types happen and each can be very bad.

Your Own Social Media Campaign Turned Against You

Companies walk a thin line with social media programs: "We want the voice of consumers to be heard! But...we don't want them to say certain things." Robust programs offer incredible tools for creation and sharing. Many are

93

backed with awareness programs to generate large levels of participation. Several prominent companies have received as much negative publicity as positive.

Chevy developed a web site where consumers could use pre-produced video segments, graphics and music to make their own commercial for the Chevy Tahoe. If a consumer liked their handiwork, they could use the power of social media to share it with friends. Unfortunately one of the capabilities within the system was custom captions. Consumer created slick, professional TV spots with phrases like, "$70 to fill up the tank, which will last less than 400 miles. Chevy Tahoe" and "Like this snowy wilderness? Better get your fill of it now. Then say hello to global warming."

American Apparel conducted an online contest to find a new featured plus size model. People could upload their own photos and the community was used to determine the winning model. A smart 24-year old from Texas submitted a series of photos that mocked the fashion establishment's view of "beauty" and "modeling." Consumers picked her. American Apparel chose not to award her the prize and the bad publicity spiraled from there.

Qantas Airlines decided to harness the power of Twitter's hashtag system by creating a simple campaign where customers were encouraged to share their "dream luxury in-flight experience." Ignoring the fact that mile high club jokes were just too easy, customers were asked to tweet their thoughts with the hashtag "#Qantas Luxury." the campaign was quickly hijacked and the hashtag was used to propagate complaints, nasty comments, jokes and horror stories.

94

Social Media Tools Used As Weapons Against Brands

One of the most famous incidences of social media being used against a company is the viral video hit "United Breaks Guitars." In 2008 Canadian musician Dave Carroll checked his guitar on a United Airlines Flight. During a stop at Chicago's O'Hare airport he alleges that he and other passengers were able to see baggage handlers THROWING guitars while transferring luggage. When he arrived at his destination he discovered that the neck of his $3,500 Taylor guitar had been broken. At different points he was told that he should not have checked it and that he should have complained sooner. After nine months of frustrating negotiations, Dave and his band produced and launched a video, "United Breaks Guitars". Since its release the video has received over 10 million views. United attempted to clumsily rectify the issue by complimenting Carrol, asking if they could use the video for customer service training and making a donation to a music institute. Although other factors were at play, United Airline's stock price fell 10%, representing $180 million in value within 4 days of the video being posted online.

The Kryptonite line of locks is well known for its durability and security. One person found it surprising when he discovered that he could open one of their U-shaped locks with a simple, disposable pen. He blogged about it. Other blogs picked it up. Even the New York Times ran a feature story. The brand did not respond.

When BP accidentally spilled million of gallons of oil into the Gulf of Mexico, its Facebook page was slammed with post after post by citizens and environmentalists. BP's posts and comments were drowned like a fish in oil. To complicate matters a fake Twitter account was created where "BP" offered updates on the situation such as "Catastophe is a strong word. Let's all agree to call it a whoopsie daisy."

In 2007 a Comcast technician visited a home to fix a modem problem. We'll ignore for the moment that Comcast missed three other appointments. He called the customer service central office for assistance and was placed on hold for over an hour. At that point he fell asleep on the couch, a moment which was captured on video and promptly uploaded. The video quickly eclipsed 1 million views and became the hallmark of poor Comcast customer service.

Ah, rats. A clip of rats jaunting through a New York City fast food restaurant was posted on YouTube. Copies and other versions went viral and quickly amassed more than 2 million views.

In an interesting example of social media dovetailing with journalism: a picture of a laptop catching fire spread through the blogoshere like, uh, wildfire after it was published on the tech news site Gizmodo.

Self-Inflicted Social Media Damage

Social media mistakes will happen. Typos, poor word choices and awkward photos may always slip through, but brands continue to miss the mark with poor attempts at humor, miscalculating relevancy, making technical mistakes, and flat out not getting it.

Summer's Eve got the bad social ball rolling when it launched an advertorial in Woman's Day magazine on how to ask for a raise. Part of the preparation they recommended? Washing your, uh, woman parts. The social world went crazy. Why exactly does a woman need to wash her "business" in order to get a raise? When it comes to the world of social media and content marketing, product placements can not feel forced.

Chrysler found that who tweets, which account is used, and what is said are all very important. A staffer posted the following tweet: "I find it ironic that Detroit is known as the #motorcity and yet no one here knows how to f------- drive." (No hyphens in the actual tweet.)

A Honda manager was caught in the act of AstroTurfing which is propping up your own brand online. After he made several posts in an attempt to diffuse negative sentiment, the social world quickly figured out who he was and made him an example of a brand attempting to misuse social media.

The Denny's restaurant chain asked people to follow them on Twitter. Unfortunately the handle they printed on their menus was for a young person from Taiwan. The misprint appeared on thousands of menus more than 1,500 Denny's restaurants across the country.

Two no-doubt, future managers of Domino's Pizza, got a giggle by videoing themselves abusing food and doing other disgusting things. The video was uploaded to You-Tube and received more than one million views before it was pulled down.

A representative from Belkin, a global computer hardware

Friends With Features & Benefits – A Marketer's Guide to Scoring with Social Media

manufacturer, was caught offering money for positive reviews.

And Just When You Think It Couldn't Get Worse

Social media has taken some very ugly and unexpected turns. Really bad guys have attempted, and succeeded, at adding malicious software code with their user generated content. And of course, disgruntled employees have circulated highly confidential information.

Don't let fear stop you from embracing the power of social media. Just use it to sharpen your thinking and plan for contingencies.

Kenneth J. Weiss

Chapter 16

Quick Bangs and Long Term Relationships

A long term strategy for creating a social smart organization is needed, not just a great short term campaign

Social media is in its nascent stage, defined by lots of "let's-try-this" moments. Brands are experimenting with a variety of different tactics. Some work. Some don't. But it's fun. Now is the time, however, to lay the foundation for long term success.

Strengthen Your Core For Better Results

The first step in having a long term social media strategy within the marketing team will be to decide how you want to build the core competency. Will you look to build an in-house resource with a high skill spike in social media, or will you build relationships with outside firms?

If you build internally, you may be subject to the "all eggs in one basket" disaster. Social media will be a hot field for the foreseeable future and good employees will be poached. When this happens, not only will you need to deal with the mechanics of log-ins and passwords, but you will also need to deal with ongoing conversations and campaigns as well as long term plans. This can be mitigated by having an internal social media team rather than a single resource, but for many companies, having a single person is a more likely budget reality. If you manage to retain your team, you will need to fight off the myopia that sometimes strikes internal departments. Plan on lots of seminars and conventions to keep the team fresh. (If you can justify a team, Chapter 17 will provide some guidelines for structuring a team.)

If you go out of house, you will face a different set of dangers. The agency or resource may hold a bias for one social tactic, they may not have the same philosophy for measurement and ROI and they, too, will be subject to employees that come and go. You will need to shop carefully. Applicable experience, fee structures and service levels will vary widely.

Creating A Social Media Culture For The Long Haul

Regardless of whether marketing leaders builds in-house or uses outside resources, they will need to constantly improve the social media acumen.

Educating Senior Management - Social media is a classic "damned if you do, damned if you don't" proposition. Senior leaders will see news stories, hear country club anecdotes, and garner advice from counterparts. You, as the social media leader will hear, "have we considered this?" "why aren't our results as good as..." and more. Make it your mission to educate senior management. As their understanding grows, the value and appreciation of social media within the organization will grow.

Create a Culture of Documentation and Measurement - Social media tends to breed fast and loose project management. Crunchy deadlines, changing requirements and user-contributed curveballs can be seen as an excuse for straying

100

from good project management. Be vigilant! Be demanding! Projects should be completely documented and measured. Each should have the proper post mortem. Develop and optimize your record keeping in a way that builds true institutional knowledge that cannot simply walk out the door when a key person leaves.

Personally Stay Current - With social media absolutely exploding in a million directions, staying current is tough. Schedule your workload to allow time for exploration and experimentation. Find some thought leaders who you like. Buy new devices and circulate them within your team. Hang out with young people. Try your hand at content creation. Doing all of this may feel like an enormous undertaking. Try taking small bites and nibble all day.

Extend Beyond Social Media For Marketing - As the marketing team builds expertise in social media, you might be asked to participate in corporate social strategies, or you may need to take it upon yourself to force the social strategy in other parts of the company. Time is tight. Budgets are tight. The staff is small. Pushing corporate social media issues may feel like the last thing you want to do. Ignore the urge to ignore it.

Educating The Entire Organization - Should accounts receivable and the maintenance staff be trained on social media? Absolutely! While they might not need the same type of training as marketing, they should know the basics (and rules) about forwarding content, making posts, commenting on a competitor's content, sharing information and more.

Fine Tune Your Management Skills - Social media, like

interactive marketing, will bring a new cast of characters to your life, and the demands of their jobs will challenge you to change the way you think about managing. If you are a weight loss company, will you want your social media efforts ramped up and well monitored on January 1st? Absolutely! What will you need to do to get the staff to work on a day that everyone else uses to relax and sober up? Some developers may have no issue pulling consecutive all nighters to meet a deadline. What will they want in return? Will you be interested in the hard-core gamer water cooler conversations or will you be hiding at your desk?

Cozy Up To Vendors - To stay informed and open-minded you'll need to take more sales calls, attend more web meetings, and see more vendor presentations than ever before. This will help you stay abreast of the latest opportunities. Yes, the vendors will beg and bug you for a chance. Just a pilot. Just a project. Think of these as one-meeting-stands with no strings attached. Learn what you can and move on. Every once in a while you may truly hit it off with a new vendor.

Make Sure HR Is Up To Speed - HR will need to cover lots of new ground in a socially-attuned organization. What will happen if you want to hire a person who has created a strong personal brand that is aligned with another company? How will the "no compete" agreement need to change? Where will researching social media and "goofing off" be demarcated? The challenges will be many, but an HR department who deals with it by refusing to deal with it will be an anchor.

Build Your Social Currency - The organization, not just the brands, should be a player in the social space. Socially smart companies will attract better employees. Employees will be drawn by the vibe, hipness and transparency.

Build Training and Knowledge Sharing Into Your Plans - Formalize training programs within the company and budget appropriately for conferences and seminars.

For more on creating an internal team...read on.

Kenneth J. Weiss

Chapter 17

Social Media Positions For More Satisfaction

Typical positions, friends of friends and how to hire

When you find the right positions, social media feels great. But what works for one company is not going to work for another. No "compu-sutra" guide exists. Titles and job descriptions are evolving, and the rapid change in technologies means that the discipline itself is changing. Just like any other field, people who excel at a tactic might not be the best leaders or strategists, and there are managers who do not know the mechanics of doing particular things.

While some companies will continue to lean on outside resources for the foreseeable future, aggressive brands are building internal staffs. Hiring is difficult. Setting goals is challenging. Measuring performance is tricky. Luckily getting it right the first time is not critical. You will need to experiment until you are satisfied.

Typical Positions

Salaries, titles, requirements and compensation are up in the air and may remain unsettled for a long period of time. Some companies think that a go-getter can do it all while being paid nothing, while other firms are building orgs with well stratified layers of VP, Director, Manager and more. Here are the typical players:

Blogger - An internal blogger might develop content for a single brand or multiple brands. Bloggers may ghost write content for senior executives, as well. Strong bloggers may even develop more advanced articles and whitepapers that can be used as part of content marketing and search engine optimization efforts. In-demand bloggers know how to capture the brand, deliver real value to the user, moderate comments and have a knack for involving the correct internal people while keeping things moving.

Social Media Strategist - A social media strategist is a person who understands marketing, knows branding, is fundamentally sound with social media and knows how to conceive programs that are realistic for budgets, logistics, timelines and results. Most importantly, the strategist needs to be just that - a strategist - not a tactician. If a person has built a few campaigns relying on a handful of tactics, they may not be a viable strategist. Also, the best strategists know how to align social media projects to satisfy short and long term objectives. They cannot be loose hammers running around looking for nails to pound.

Content Curator - Consumers in today's social media world want content that delivers true value, not simply rehashed brand statements and advertising. Generating, collecting and clearing content takes time. Content curators work with internal resources to generate content, find and secure content from third party sources, manage rights issues and facilitate a well-organized and strategically relevant content repository. This can be as simple as posting links of interests and as complex as working with dozens of global teams to develop well-structured, on-brand content. Content curators must understand users, good writing, internal technical systems and how to develop chunks and teasers that work in the social world.

Account/Channel Manager - These pros may be aligned along two dimensions: They can be assigned to a particular brand or operating unit, or they may have primary responsibility for a social media site (or channel) for one or many brands. A typical example is one person holding the keys to a company's YouTube account. In a situation such as this that person can really dig into and stay up to date on a property. While there will always be generalists, seasoned marketers know that people can build incredibly deep and rich skill sets around disciplines such as identity development, direct response copy development, etc. The same will ultimately hold true for individual social media tactics.

Community Manager - The scope and structure of communities can vary greatly. Media sites, portals and even large brands can have communities with hundreds or thousands of participants. A B2B firm by contrast may have a message board with a small, but very high value audience.

Content Developer/Producer - Social media is not a "read only" media. Consumers want to watch videos, interact with content, see tons of photos, listen to podcasts and more. A content producer needs to understand what consumers feel is valuable and know how to create (or source) multiple content types. Even a basic social media program will require a steady stream of new content.

Project Manager, Producer - Good social media producers have bullet-proof project management skills and an acute ability to understand what is technically possible. A producer typically oversees multiple ongoing projects while working with diverse resources from designers to developers. At the end of the day the PM/Producer is responsible for delivering on time.

Content Manager - A content manager lives with one foot in the world of strategy and the other in the world of execution. The manager needs to continually ensure that newly developed content assets are strategically appropriate while all schedules are being maintained.

Writers, Editors and Proofreaders - Depending upon the size of the social media effort, the writing staff can be any size. Programs that rely on a steady stream of content creation, posts across numerous venues and other copy intensive efforts will require multiple people, or people capable of wearing multiple hats. The team will need to work quickly and effectively to meet the demands of "right now" social media consumers.

Programs Manager and Administrators - When programs become increasingly complex with user activities, multiple parts, award components and more, program managers are necessary. For example, a company running a large scale blogger outreach program or brand ambassador program will need a dedicated resource at some point.

Analyst - Analyzing social media programs should not simply be a matter of copying data from reporting tools. Analysts need to look at trends over time, filter anomalies, use appropriate benchmarking data, understand the impact of external marketing campaigns and bring insight and information to the organization, not just data points. Analysts should be involved in projects from the very beginning to ensure that ROI models are created and can be accurately executed with the data being generated by the programs. Remember, if a system is not configured to generate or capture certain types of data, recreating an accurate picture after the fact becomes impossible.

Developers/Technologists - Social media programs are going to require the support of sound developers and technologists. Companies quickly find that what they want to execute or analyze is not always possible with existing social media systems. Tweaking is needed. Data will need to be moved. Digital experiences will need to be created. Social experiences must be connected.

Social Media Advocate/Coach - Evangelizing the possibilities of social media throughout an organization while balancing optimism and realism is essential. Coaches should not be marketing-centric. Rather, they should have a point of view on social media's ability to affect the different component of a business. Sometimes this person is a cheerleader. Other times this person will rain on parades. The goal is to interest and invigorate the organization without creating unrealistic expectations.

Other People You'll Attract

Social media teams and experts need to continually build a network of specialized resources. As the social media bar gets nudged higher and higher, projects will need a little bit of something extra to stay competitive, let alone stand out from the crowd.

3D Modelers and Animators - How about a slick, animated webisode? Perhaps an animation of your product at work? What about assets for an augmented reality experience? You will have more of these ideas than you think, and many of them will require a modeler or animator.

Game Designers and Developers - People love games. Simple, casual games. Massive multi-player games. They will pay for some and expect others for free. You can be certain, though, that people know good games from bad games. In order to develop solid games, you will need the help of a seasoned pro.

App Developers - Let's jump to the end for one second. If you are going to develop an app, you will need to have a plan for building awareness, interest and intent. Otherwise, your app-venture will be a technical exercise only. Now back to the beginning: App developers are alchemists that can take the attributes of a brand, the motivations of consumers and a slew of technology to develop a fulfilling, compact experience. Just like games, consumers can quickly tell a good app from a bad one.

Video Editors/Motion Graphics Specialists/Producers - These people can range from freelancers with killer desktop systems to full blown studios. The projects might be as simple as "let's edit last year's product video to remove a few shots" or as complicated as "let's create an eye-catching opening sequence for all of our YouTube videos." Pricing for these projects will vary widely as well.

Familiar Faces

The interactive "basics" of usability, system performance, information architecture, conversion optimization and user experience cannot be overlooked when it comes to social media. Let's face it, many companies are not getting these right in their basic digital initiatives. Social media is just another place where these problems occur, it is not a place to hide from these issues. To get them right you will need some to tap some "traditional" digital pros.

User Experience (UX) Strategist/Architect - Good UX people are worth their weight in gold. They understand branding, usability and delivering experiences that satisfy users' needs while advancing the brand.

Information Architects - Woe is the company that begins executing social media projects by looking at layouts and mockups. Information architects are masters of flow diagrams and experience diagrams that prescribe how the system should behave. These specialists help ensure that everything people find frustrating is eliminated as early as possible from the project.

Application Developers - These people are a slightly different breed than App Developers. Think of an application developer as a person capable of creating a software program that lets users do something. This can be something like, "we want people to be able to shop and checkout right from our Facebook page." Or, "Let's create a social powered freelance marketplace so people can sell their services." These are not simple "programs" and the complexity is raised as privacy, financial, transactional and backend integration requirements are added to the mix.

111

Flash Developers - Flash is an amazing technology and vastly underestimated and appreciated by the general business public. Although some browsers and devices do not support the technology, it is an essential piece of Internet goo that makes the web and social media active, vibrant and interactive. Good Flash developers think beyond simple interactivity to a genre that combines the best of Hollywood, Harvard and Old Havana.

Typical Team Building Mistakes

Building a social media team is not easy. Try to avoid these typical mistakes.

Underpaying - Since businesses are not sure of the ROI or the true long-term strategic value, the tendency to underpay is prevalent. Lower compensation packages are going to attract the less qualified.

Being Too Tool Centric - Companies sometimes mistake mastery of a single tool with the ability to run an entire social media program. Just because a person has amassed a huge Twitter following or managed a company's YouTube channel for a year does not make them an ideal candidate.

Overestimating Zeal While Underestimating Experience - Young superstars who "get it" will always exist. They can be found in music, art, business, and yes, social media. However, not every young person with zeal will be a social media superstar.

Funding the Position But Not The Activity - Social media is not free. You will need to develop content and create experiences. If you want specialized tasks like video editing or animation done in house, you will need to invest in technology. Having a social media person in house with no budget is a recipe for disaster.

The Odd Bundle - If you read social media job descriptions, the companies that do not understand it are apparent. These are the companies that lump all types of mismatched tasks together such as social media, search engine optimization and customer service.

Underestimating The Time Commitment - Have you seen this advertisement? "We're looking for a part time person 10-15 hours per week to handle the social media activities of our three keystone brands..." This is a company that clearly does not understand the difference between a true social media campaign and using a single social media tool.

Lack of Training - The rate of change in social media is not slowing anytime soon. Companies will need to provide access to training for the staff.

Kenneth J. Weiss

Chapter 18

You'll Need to Have Some Standards

Web standards, brand guidelines, editorial style guides and legal guidance

Companies who have employees that embrace social media become more socially savvy companies. Sounds simple, correct? But how can a company regulate behavior in a way that provides the right amount of legal protection and ensures productivity while encouraging trial and exploration? Legal battles between companies and their employees are already popping up around the country over the ownership of blogs, the use of certain screen names, comments made by employees and more.

Today's always-connected, always-on world makes crafting social media policies even more difficult. When is an employee acting as an agent of the company? What happens if they post after hours? What happens if it is after hours on a personal account, but from a company smart phone? The lines are really blurry.

The key to sound policy is having social media thinking incorporated into your existing standards and having specific social media documents.

Health Check Your Existing Documents

Begin by auditing your existing standards and documentation through the lens of social media.

Brand Guidelines - Brands survive and thrive by staying on brand. Straying from the script weakens brands and can damage the legal viability of marks and brand elements. One component of brand has always been tonality. (This can include elements of voice and personality.) Brands need to determine how that tonality will work in a social space that is quicker, more conversational and prone to shorthand and emoticons. Should a world-renowned hospital use a phrase like "OMG!" in a post? Your brand standards should also provide guidance on naming accounts and setting up new accounts on emerging properties.

Workflow and Approval - In most organizations, anything that publicly represents a brand is subject to a strict approval and sign-off process. Will that work when the brand's Facebook administrator notices a negative post at 1AM that could be diffused with a fast response?

Visual Language and Visual Style Guides - Image conscious brands usually have defined visual language and style guides. Would these by default preclude a company from embracing different types of user generated content? Imagine an appliance manufacturer running a contest for people to submit their own designs. What would the brand do with a great idea that fell outside of the visual language? Would a brand want ideas floating around the Internet carrying their logo, that did not look like their carefully scripted style?

Beautiful, fashion-driven images are also fueling sites like Pinterest. Should a brand expand its photo styles to include images that would resonate with this mind set?

Legal Guidelines - Legal issues surrounding social media can fill an entire book. From a marketing and legal standpoint, one simple question can lead to head scratching and paralysis: "What is a claim?" When an employee posts a comment or uploads a video about a product, when does it pass from being puffery to being a claim that can be defended with a rigorous, standardized test? Companies have spent hundreds of millions of dollars going to battle over claims. Social media statements are likely to lead to more battles. Your legal counsel will need to get up to speed quickly and be responsive enough to keep pace with an active social media program.

Editorial Guidelines - These guidelines have traditionally governed how sanctioned writers within an organization develop content that is used to promote a company. What happens when dozens or hundreds of people within an organization (whose titles have nothing to do with writing or editing) begin to create content that is exposed to the public? Are they subject to the guidelines? Do the guidelines cover only what would usually be considered an article? Or do they cover all types of content like a sales support engineer doing a simple stand-up video in a conference room to explain a tricky assembly step?

Business Conduct Guidelines - People acting as an agent of the company are expected to conduct the affairs of the company in a particular way. Can social media short circuit those? If a potential vendor sends a Linkedin request to a person during an RFP process, would that constitute an uneven playing field? What happens if it is accepted?

Your Social Media Policy Needs To Be Ready For Three Audiences

For some, social media policies will need to direct three groups: those within your social media program, employees involved in social media who are not a part of the program, and outside people who are participants in the program.

Guiding Your Social Media Programs - Your social media programs should start with a mission statement. Yes, mission statements are sometimes ridiculous and ambiguous, but with so much of the social world changing each day, some high level, conceptual agreement is needed. How responsive will you be? How much transparency is necessary? How committed is the organization to training and experimentation? How will you change the corporate, day-to-day schedule to excel within the 24-hour world of social media? Think big. Be bold. Believe in your brand and what it stands for. Get other people to share it and love it passionately and let them be participants and advocates.

Once you have agreement on the foundational elements, you will need to decide on your more tactical approach to running campaigns. How will you insist on and develop strategies? What will be your approach for setting objectives and measuring? Will you report the failures as completely as the successes? What will be your approach to involving and coaching key stakeholders and subject matter experts? How will you keep your team up to speed with all corporate documentation? You will also need rock-solid procedures for managing user names and passwords. You will need to determine specific workflows, standardize documentation and develop procedures for monitoring your reputation and tracking competitors.

And, don't forget your vendors and contractors. They should know what you are willing to accept and which places are out of bounds.

Guiding Employees Not Formally Involved In Social Media Programs - Since everyone in your entire organization has access to social media either through work systems, smart phones or home computers, you will need to make EVERYONE aware of your policies.

- Astroturfing - This little faux pas is attempting to support an idea or brand by pretending to be a consumer or member of the community instead of divulging your affiliation with an organization. Many employees are tempted to give high ratings or make positive comments about a product from their accounts. In some companies, this is actually encouraged. What will your policy be? Since other companies do it (sometimes in a highly orchestrated fashion) will your organization implicitly encourage it, prohibit it, or just look the other way?

- Commenting about the Competition - Although some employees get nervous here, many have no problems firing social bullets at the competition. Is it okay if they do it from home? How about if they log in to a personal account from work and let the salvos fly?

- User and Account Names - You will need to specifically outline under what conditions a company name or brand can be used as part of a user or account name.

- Ownership of Accounts - People in R&D, Quality, Customer Service and more are likely to start social media accounts during their tenure with the company. Under what circumstances are the accounts personal, and under what circumstances are they owned by the company?

- Responding to Posts - When a negative post directly attacks a company or brand, who is entitled to respond? Many passionate employees have no reservations about diving in, and many social experiences let anyone (including internal people) make comments.

- Copyright and Fair Use - Where is the line between fair use, sharing and representing ownership? Copyright issues can get messy and potentially expensive.

- Trolling - Under what circumstances can a second, "throw away" ID be created just to make a comment or post?

Guiding Outside Resources Such As Bloggers and Ambassadors - Part of any social media program is getting people to help spread the word. Some of these relationships can become more structured in the form of sponsorships or ambassador programs. Since there may be some form of compensation involved these can get tricky. You will need participant's actions to be bullet-proof when it comes to FTC regulations. They will need clear guidance on your expectations about the relationship.

Sure, having standards is not a sexy part of social media, but having standards is absolutely necessary. These guidelines will also need to be made living and collaborative. Changes will always be needed and people will want to have input.

120

Chapter 19

Don't Forget to Experiment When Moving Beyond Experimentation

It may not feel right, but you've got to keep trying new things

Social media is like college: everyone indulges in a little experimentation. However, if social media is to thrive in the business world, is it necessary to act a little more buttoned-up? Yes and no. You can experiment as long as you do it in a certain way.

Your Social Media Portfolio

In order to set the stage for experimentation, you will need to determine your appetite for experimenting. You will need to balance your approach to include tried, proven tactics with new activities that have home run potential.

The Basics, 70% - 80% - The core of your program should be made up of the basics. These are the Social Media 101 programs of Facebook, YouTube, Twitter, Pinterest, etc. Don't be fooled! Each has tremendous opportunities for innovation, but this is the area where you practice basic blocking and tackling. These programs are based upon solid execution, and you want to make your budget dollars work hard here. Nothing in this arena should command a premium price.

Enhanced Programs, 25% - 10% - This is where you take your proven winners and build upon their success with twists and turns to make them more unique, more synonymous with the brand and more endearing to your community. Expect to think a little more, and spend a little more here in order to differentiate yourself from the competition and carve a more unique space in the social world.

Explosive Experimentation: 5% -10% - This is the segment where breakthrough thinking and work can thrive. But, there are no guarantees. You will spend relatively more time and money here. You will learn a tremendous amount. Be prepared for failure as well as success. You may also need to let some of your most trusted resources focus on this area for a prolonged period of time in order to find something amazing.

How To Experiment

Experimenting is not randomly groping in the dark, although there is a time and place for that, too. In order to experiment in the social media space, you will need to adopt a practiced approach.

Having a Defined Learning Objective - Only bad organizations spend money "just to see what happens." You should have a distinct hypothesis or defined learning objective for each of your pilots. Everyone, from senior marketing management to team members should clearly understand the learning objective.

What is the Worst Case Scenario? - Things can go wrong. The degree of acceptable pain is the issue. You will need to be incredibly transparent about the possible worst case scenario.

Know How To Stop - If a project goes into a horrific nosedive, how will you extricate yourself from the situation? This is a tough one, because big chunks of experience and content that flow from a project may be irretrievable. Your ability to "stop" a program may not really exist.

Measure - Think ahead! You will not be able to measure certain aspects of your experiment unless measurement is engineered into the original solution and experience. Many people have been burned by hinging their analysis on a data point that the experience was never able to capture. Hedge your bets by planning on measuring everything.

Concept for Scalability - Good experiments are those that can be scaled up to create a larger total return on the investment. This can be involving more people, increasing the interaction with the same number of people, generating more data, delivering more sales, etc. Small can be okay, but having something that can grow is better.

Repeatable - If you cannot repeat the fundamental experience and results of a program, you are condemned to chasing one hit wonders. That is a career destined for failure. Part of the inherent value of experiments is being able to repeat the success. If nothing else, the fundamental framework and philosophy should be repeatable.

Document Everything - Social media experimentation should not be like cooking without a recipe. Everything that is done, and everything that happens should be meticu-

Friends With Features & Benefits – A Marketer's Guide to Scoring with Social Media

lously documented. Ideally, you will want these projects to slide down to your basics where less tenured and less expensive resources can execute the plan, allowing for more valuable resources to continue with experimentation.

Expect the Unexpected - Things might go unexpectedly well. Are you prepared to react and interact when things explode? Unmanaged success can be as brand damaging as mismanaged failure.

How To Build A Culture of Experimentation

Solid, experimental practices must be injected into every part of your culture.

Let Everyone Be Engaged, But Make Someone Responsible - Good ideas can come from anyone, anywhere. However, someone needs to sort through the ideas and carry the torch on the execution of the chosen ones. Make sure it is clear to the entire team who is responsible for experimentation.

Budget Money, People and Resources Accordingly - Don't expect your team to experiment and innovate if the workload has them buried each day. Also, do not point to an incredibly cool augmented reality experience and say "we should have done this" unless you have provided the budget to support those types of projects.

Develop A Process - From ideation to execution, you should have a process for flowing experimentation through the organization. Nobody wants to get fired because senior management was "surprised" and nobody wants to appear less innovative because an idea they submitted got lost in the shuffle.

Set Objectives - Even though the outcome of experimentation can be undefined, that does not mean the process or philosophy of experimentation should be devoid of objectives. Make sure this facet of your business is managed aggressively and everyone knows how success will be determined.

Make Observation Essential - Study everything about social media including what the competitors do, new technology advents and success stories in different verticals. The social world is loaded with tons of talent. Your breakthrough idea may be somebody's day-old donut.

Know How To Connect The Dots - In the end, social media experiments should roll up to your greater social media strategy, to your greater marketing strategy and to the greater business strategy. Projects that do none of those are fun, but provide no long term value.

Consider The Newbies - Bring new, younger people into your circle with some regularity. Younger people help drive social media and their insight is invaluable.

Avoid Cloning - Don't get too homogeneous in your thinking. Yes, you need some level of consensus and workplace harmony, but people with different thought processes and attitudes can help drive innovation.

Stay Tech Savvy - Buy new devices and rotate them through the staff. Challenge a local college fraternity to a gaming tournament. Take the team to Best Buy for a hands-on session. Do anything! Stay current.

Make Failing Legitimate - Sure, companies say that it is okay to fail, but employees do not always believe that since performance evaluations and bonus structures are lurking in the corner.

If you believe failure is fine, make it part of the documented objectives and measurement plan.

Listen to Your Customers - Not just in the big, esoteric ways. Spend some time every month listening to calls from your call center or monitor online chat sessions. Your customers will never feel so real to you as when you do this. It is a great way to see through the lens of the customer.

Think Big! - Ask yourself powerful questions! Develop evaluation criteria that is challenging! Don't settle for little ideas and little experiments. Put your team in a position to create game-changing ideas.

Look Outside of Categories and the Country - Look at other product categories and industries to see what's being tried. Look to international markets as well. Lots of bright people are trying different things.

Like A Boss

If you want your team to experiment, you need to lead.

Believe It - Teams can sense if your heart is not in it.

Inspire - Create the right physical environment. Buy interesting products, toys and magazines.

Share - Find interesting digital executions and circulate them.

Knock Down Obstacles - Find out what's holding back your team. Then, take care of it.

Make It a Hobby - This is not a nine-to-five phenomenon. You'll need to do it at night and on the weekends to be any good.

128

Kenneth J. Weiss

Chapter 20

It Might Feel Funny
You'll feel funny, but you need to get started

You'll find no secrets here.

At first it will feel a little funny, but in the end you may really like it.

That's it. Stop reading. Go do it.

Friends With Features & Benefits – A Marketer's Guide to Scoring with Social Media

www.ingramcontent.com/pod-product-compliance
Lightning Source LLC
Chambersburg PA
CBHW032004190326
41520CB00007B/355